YOUR RULES ARE DUMB

D1736057

YOUR RULES ARE DUMB

HOW TO MAINTAIN YOUR PARENTAL AUTHORITY WHILE CREATING A PARTNERSHIP WITH YOUR SPIRITED CHILD

REBECAH FREELING

Wits' End Parenting
info@witsendparenting.com
www.witsendparenting.com

Disclaimer
Disclaimer and Terms of Use: All efforts have been made to ensure the accuracy of the information contained in this book as of the date published; and the methods described herein are based in part on the author's extensive experience with kids. On the other hand, this book is not intended as an exhaustive treatment of the subject. No liability is assumed for errors or omissions; and no liability is assumed for losses or damages resulting from application of the information provided. Readers applying the ideas contained in this book assume full responsibility for their actions and results. Any perceived slights of specific persons, peoples, or organizations are unintentional. While all the stories in this book are true, some names and identifying details have been changed to protect the privacy of the people involved.

Your rules are dumb : how to maintain your parental authority while creating a partnership with your spirited child / Rebecah Freeling. —1st ed.

ISBN 978-0-69207-074-1

TESTIMONIALS

"[With] years of experience with families, Rebecah Freeling understands what makes 'spirited' children tick and how [these kids] are different from the 'easy' kids. She has figured out how to balance two essential yet contradictory components of childrearing: how to gain compliance and how to honor children's wishes... Whether you've just started, are discouraged, or are tearing your hair due to the daunting task of raising a spirited child, you need this important book."

–Helen F. Neville, BS RN,
author of Temperament Tools: Working With Your Child's
Inborn Traits

"It was refreshing to read Rebecah Freeling's clear and engaging approach to help[ing] teachers and parents alike work positively with intense children. Her experience and insight help...both adults and young ones to communicate with clarity and love. Thank you, Rebecah!"

–Linda Williams, PhD,
Class Teacher, Detroit Waldorf School

"As a licensed therapist who works with children and families, I have high praise for Rebecah Freeling. Her warm and unique style...brings resolution and harmony [to families]... And her sense of humor is amazing!"

–Gina Mendicino,
Licensed Marriage & Family Therapist in
San Francisco, California

"There are a lot of child behavior experts and a lot of theories about how best to develop our kids and get the family life we want. No expert has advice that's never been heard before, but Rebecah Freeling integrates the best of several approaches in a way that's wonderfully balanced, practical, and empowering. [Ms. Freeling] really 'gets' kids...and helps parents...understand their children in a unique way."

–Tamina Isolani-Nagarvala,
Physician in Oakland, California

"Rebecah Freeling is like the child whisperer!"

–Eleese Meschery,
parent of a spirited kid

Please Accept My Gift to You!

Free Temperament Assessment ($400 value)

To help you understand your child better. This will ease your stress and frustration and it will help you to give your kids what they need to thrive!

Kids are not "blank slates," and not all kids are the same. You know that your kids have their own personality, but a formal assessment of your child's temperament will give you even more insight. It will help you to better understand your child, and it will help you to

- understand why your child does what he does
- understand which of your child's behaviors are normal and which are not
- not take "bad" behavior personally
- be more patient
- see the world from your child's perspective
- understand what motivates and inspires your child

Go to http://witsendparenting.com/tempassess to get started!

To Peggy Tripp, who was my fifth-grade teacher at Benjamin Beswick Elementary School in Tustin, California. Thank you for seeing me for who I am. Wherever you are, I hope that the love and joy you gave me is now echoing back to you many, many times over.

CONTENTS

ACKNOWLEDGMENTS

First and foremost I'd like to acknowledge and thank Kirsten Enriquez, my partner in every sense of the word. She had the daunting task of getting these ideas out of my head and onto paper. Her commitment to consistency, truth and clarity is the reason this book could finally come together.

I'd also like to acknowledge Mary Sheedy Kurcinka, who introduced the world to the "Spirited Child."

Finally, I am also grateful to all the spirited children I've met and will continue to meet. These kids both inspire and infuriate me :) Truly, spirited kids are the reason I have hope for the future of humanity.

INTRODUCTION

"My nature is that I don't listen very well. I'm very determined, and I believe in myself... Thank God for that. I don't let anything stand in my way."

–Chantal Sutherland

When 4-year-old Mark's grandmother enrolled him in my preschool, she let me know: "He just hits people for no reason, and runs into people, trying to knock them over." She hoped that Mark would thrive in my school (it had a huge natural outdoor space), but she would understand if I had to expel him. In the meantime she was getting him evaluated to see if he had some kind of mental illness and was also looking for a therapist who could help him with the trauma he'd been through in his parents' home.

Mark HATED having to follow the routines of the classroom. As soon as he entered my class he began to run back and forth throughout the room; he wrecked the other kids' projects; and he also hit the teachers. So I herded him out into the yard where he could run around freely without hurting anyone.

In our yard we had open space to run in, trees to climb, a huge sandbox, and raspberry bushes planted along the fence. And of all the options that existed outside, Mark chose the raspberry bushes. He dove in, sat with his back to the fence – and only then realized what he had done. But he kept screaming, "Leave me alone!" So I left him alone. I didn't talk to him. I just picked up a rake and started in on some yard work. I remained in his line of sight and close enough that he could hear me hum softly as I worked, calm and cool as a cucumber, while he continued to scream and cuss.

After about 20 minutes, Mark screamed, "Teacher! I can't get out!"

I said, "You're stuck in the raspberry bushes."

Then Mark began to cry, no longer screaming. Sadness took over where anger left off. I continued to rake and hum quietly for another five minutes while he cried.

Mark sobbed, "Get me out."

I said, "We can work together. Would you like to do that?"

"Yes."

"OK, I'll move the raspberries aside with the rake and you can climb out. Then we'll sit on the bench and talk."

"OK."

Mark climbed out, surveyed the damage to his arms quietly, and we sat on a bench together. I didn't say anything.

He said, "I don't want to be here."

I said, "You don't want to be here. That's frustrating."

"I hate this school."

"You hate this school."

"What do you do here?"

"We work together."

"Oh. How do you do that?"

"Would you like to learn?"

"Yeah."

That was the beginning of a long and difficult road for Mark. He had to reconcile his need to be in control at every moment with the reality that he lived on a planet with other humans. There were many days when I had to lead him to the yard, as often he needed to run and rage before he could work together with us.

But by the time he left my school, Mark was a compassionate, creative leader. He came to understand how his body worked, how to use it constructively, and how to express his deep anger and sadness without hurting other people. In problem-solving sessions, he came up with interesting, intelligent solutions to all kinds of problems. And he appreciated the opportunity to use his mind to gain the control he so desperately wanted.

Mark is the quintessential "spirited" child. He had a great deal of power and a very strong will. At first he absolutely hated to work with others. He had backed himself against a wall, he had barricaded himself with thorns, he was screaming to be left alone – but he longed to be led out of his predicament. And it's not easy to help a child in that situation. *How* you help is crucial. To lead spirited kids out of the thorns, we must be willing to listen and collaborate. The helper's tone of voice is paramount. The helper's mood must be positive, hopeful and open. Also, I had to honor the fact that Mark was who he was for a very good reason. I had to wait for him to request help, and I also had to hold him accountable for his actions.

Spirited kids have amazing strength and potential. And parents and teachers have an amazing opportunity to help them create incredible lives with that strength, if we are courageous, steadfast and unrelenting, just like they are.

* * *

My name is Rebecah Freeling. I am a child behavior expert and parent coach. I specialize in energetic, intense, strong-willed, won't-take-No-for-an-answer, "spirited" kids; and I wrote this book to provide parenting advice to parents of these kids.

I've worked with a lot of kids over the years, and I intend to equip you, empower you – and encourage you. In this book I'll be sharing some techniques that I've found to be key to developing an effective working relationship with your spirited child. But even more important, I'll be sharing a parenting mindset and encouraging a perspective-shift that can dramatically reduce your frustration and stress. This mindset will also help you to parent in the true sense of the word: It will make it easier for you to work with your child as a teacher, trainer, and mentor. Because that's what raising kids is all about, right? We want to nurture them and we want them to know they're loved, but we also want to equip and prepare them to thrive as adults.

What I have to share is based on my experience with many, many kids and their parents. But before I get started, let me tell you a little about the path that brought me to where I am today.

My Journey

I've noticed and paid attention to the process of teaching ever since I was a young girl. And when I was a kid I was aware that some of my teachers really connected with me and the other kids, and some of them didn't. I remember in particular my fourth-grade teacher, who didn't think I was nearly as clever as I actually was, and I got lots of notes sent home that year.

Math was especially troublesome, because I thought math could be a really interesting story about how the numbers all related to each other. We were doing fractions and I thought it was so interesting when the big number was on the top and the little number was on the bottom. And if the little number didn't want so much on top and the top was too heavy the little number could slide some of it off so that the number on top could become smaller than the little number on the bottom. But when I tried to explain improper fractions to the class this way, my teacher said, "Rebecah, this is math class, not storytelling." Another note sent home.

But the next year I had a teacher who was able to connect with every one of her students and I immediately intuited this – that she totally "got" me and every other kid in the class. And I watched the way she responded to everybody as individuals and I thought, "That's what I want to do. I want to be a teacher." And so it was that teacher who inspired me and made me want to work with kids and connect with them in the way she connected with me.

So fast-forward many years, and I've started an early-childhood center in Columbus, Ohio, where I attempted to do just that: establish a genuine, strong connection with each child who enrolled. And I like to say that this resulted in my attracting more than my share of what we are now calling "spirited" kids – the ones who have "too much" energy, they may be aggressive, they're often in trouble at home and at school. I'd have 3- or 4-year-olds who had already been kicked out of two or three preschools! And in my school, which was called Briar Rose Children's Center, no one ever got kicked out, everyone learned what the State said they needed to know to move to the next grade, and most important, everyone learned the self-discipline they needed to function "appropriately" in the world around them. And now some of these kids are doing some amazing things. One of my kids, now a teenager, extended a consequence she received as a result of forbidden partying to include raising hundreds of dollars for the local food bank that had supported her family in her younger years. Another just biked across Spain. Another is training to be an Olympic swimmer.

In 2011 I closed Briar Rose and my partner and I moved to the West Coast. And once I got settled I decided to quit teaching in the school context and instead focus more directly on what I enjoy most – helping to solve the behavior- and parent-child relationship problems that cause so much stress to so many families. I began to work with kids and their parents as a family coach, and now my team and I provide other services to families as well.

A SUMMARY OF WHAT'S COMING: ESSENTIALLY, IT COMES DOWN TO TWO THINGS...

I said above that this book is intended to give parenting advice. In particular, this book shows you what you should do to manage, leverage, and transform your spirited kid's problem behavior. And I've learned that the most effective response to spirited kids' problem behavior amounts to two basic strategies. One, parents need to establish themselves as the ones in charge of the family. And two, parents should share their decision-making power with their child, and relate to their child as a partner and collaborator.

This may sound like a paradox, and if it does, think about a team captain, or the team's coach. Everyone's in the game, everyone has the same goal, but these folks lead the team. The first part of this book (Chapters 2 and

3) focuses on parents being in charge, because – due to the child's place in the course of human development – you can't develop a truly collaborative relationship with your child unless you first establish yourself as a leader she's willing to follow. The second half of this book (Chapters 4 and 5) focuses more directly on collaboration itself, providing perspectives and one key strategy that will help you to partner with your child in an effective and empowering way.

And in Chapter 1 I summarize some of the key assumptions that underlie my approach to parenting. These are my assumptions, and I hope they'll become your assumptions too – because ultimately, working with spirited kids is about perspective, and it's about the two broad strategies I described above. In other words, this book is not an index of parenting tips, although I *do* talk about a few techniques in great detail. But parenting spirited kids is much more effective and much less frustrating if you start with an empowered perspective as to who these kids are and how they work.

1

Start With These Assumptions

"Spirited kids don't want to be 'good.'"

–Rebecah Freeling

Working with spirited kids is about much more than technique. Ultimately, if you really want to parent in the true sense of the word – if you want to raise your spirited kid to be high-functioning, to be happy, and to reach his incredible potential – you need to start with mindset. Here are some of the main assumptions that underlie my work with spirited kids. I hope you'll adopt them, too!

Assumption #1: There's nothing wrong with your child.

Most of the parents who seek my help want to change their child's "bad" behavior. "My child won't do anything I say," they tell me. "She has three-hour-long tantrums, she kicks she bites she hits, everything's an argument, she's in trouble at school." And despite today's much more permissive approach to behaviors that would have gotten me grounded for eternity when I was a kid, many of my parents think there's got to be something wrong with their kid. They have friends, they talk, their kid is not like other kids – *and their kid does not respond to distractions or rewards or consequences the way other kids do.*

So one piece of my message to parents and teachers is that there's nothing wrong with these kids. This message is not new, of course. Other child-behavior experts, like Mary Sheedy Kurcinka, author of *Raising Your Spirited Child*, have also attempted to normalize "spirited," strong-willed behavior. Still, there are a whole lot of doctors and therapists diagnosing these same kids with ADHD or Oppositional Defiant Disorder. And I've learned that, whether the child has a diagnosis or not, the vast majority of the time their behavior stems from their temperament – and you can transform the behavior with education and training. I also believe that a lot of what we think is wrong with these kids is exactly what the world needs today.

ASSUMPTION #2: WE NEED SPIRITED KIDS — BECAUSE WE NEED "SPIRITED," STRONG-WILLED ADULTS.

Unlike many child behavior experts who want to normalize spirited kids' behavior mainly for the sake of "taming" it, I am passionate in my belief that strong-willed, energetic, impulsive, sensitive, incredibly persistent, often very smart kids are the ones best suited to solve the incredible challenges we're facing today.

Wholesale destruction of the environment. Widespread poverty, hunger, violence and war. The undermining of democracy and civil liberties, not only in other countries, but also in our own. Global financial instability and the ever-widening gap between the rich and the poor; the impoverishment of the middle-class.

Hey, we need people who are strong-willed. We need people who won't take No for an answer. We need people who won't let any obstacle stand in their way. We need people who are going to do it no matter what a corrupt authority says. Of course, a strong-willed kid isn't necessarily going to grow up to be a helpful problem-solver – we have to lead him to that. But leading him to that is so much more effective when we embrace his temperament and personality as the strengths they actually are. I even like to view his problem behaviors as undeveloped strengths (more on this in Chapter 4). And when parents can shift their perspective and see these problem behaviors as undeveloped strengths, the *problem* becomes much smaller – and the behavior becomes a teaching opportunity:

Assumption #3: Parenting is much easier when you see yourself as your child's primary teacher.

If you focus mainly on stopping bad behavior, parenting is an uphill battle. But if you focus less on the behavior problem and more on developing and empowering your child, parenting is an awesome opportunity.

Wait a minute, many of you are saying. My kid is so impulsive, so volatile, so oppositional – I don't care about any "opportunity." I just really, really need him to stop. OK, don't get me wrong. Stopping bad behavior goes a long,

long way toward reducing stress and conflict in your home. And as you'll see, I believe that holding kids accountable for their behavior is crucial. So I'm not talking about parenting techniques, here; I'm talking about a perspective shift – an important one. *Because if your intention is mainly to stop the bad behavior, your burden will feel much heaver and you'll miss out on the relief and hope and strength that come when you fully embrace your role as teacher, guide, and coach.*

And I do mean, fully embrace this role. I'm not just parroting that often-stated rationalization: "Her behavior is simply a lack of skills..." Instead, I'm asking you to, whenever she misbehaves, slow down and remind yourself that your job is to use that misbehavior as a chance to develop her. Keep it at the front of your awareness: She's not here just because your family wanted another person to love. She is also here to learn from you and you are here to coach and develop her, to empower her to thrive and to reach her potential in a very difficult world. Teaching turns problems into opportunities, and when you think about it, doesn't "teaching" and "empowering" feel more positive and less stressful than "fixing a big problem"? Spirited kids' behavior *can* seem like a big problem at times, but if you show them how to get their needs met in productive ways, you turn those problems into valuable gifts. And this brings me to another key assumption:

ASSUMPTION #4: SPIRITED KIDS DO NOT WANT TO BE "GOOD." INSTEAD, THEY WANT AUTONOMY — THEY WANT THE FREEDOM TO CHOOSE WHAT'S IMPORTANT TO THEM.

Your kid does not want to be good? OK, I'm overstating it, a little. I am not saying that your child has absolutely no desire to cooperate with you. But we all differ when it comes to personality and temperament. Some of us are more introverted or more easygoing, for example. And some of us are more "service-oriented," more willing to cooperate (we may have a higher need for others' approval) – *and some of us are much less so.*

And when you understand that strong-willed, spirited kids are highly driven by their own ideas and plans, and less inclined to forego those plans in service of someone else's, this provides a new perspective on their behavior – and on what works to shape that behavior. For example: If you assume that a child naturally wants to be good, you're going to do what one teacher did with a spirited child who was regularly disruptive during rest time: "Lucy, all of your friends are resting now. See? This is what we're supposed to be doing right now." If Lucy wanted to be a good girl, she would think, "Oh, yeah. I should obey the teacher the way my friends are doing, drop my toy, and lie down." Instead, she thought, "Well, rest time is dumb! *Those* kids can rest. I have things to do." And then she proceeded to do them – which is why that teacher called me...

Let's face it, if strong-willed kids were highly motivated to please, sticker charts would work with them. Because that chart means more than attractive rewards or undesired consequences – to kids, it's also a clear statement about what, to parents, are the desired ("good") and undesired ("bad") behaviors. And speaking of rewards, let me be clear: My point is not simply that your kid is not a people-pleaser – our main concern is with what *does* motivate him.

I've said that he desires autonomy, but why does he want this? Again, a lot of is temperament. But it's also very helpful if you can really get just how smart, curious, creative and energetic he is, and how much these factors drive him. The psychological and neurological evidence give us some insight into kids' high-intensity thought life: Children's brains are much more active and more creative than adults' brains: The 3-year-old brain is actually twice as active. Your kid is exploring, thinking, creating, planning – and when a child who's full of energy and great ideas is also less inclined to please, this child can present as oppositional. But he isn't. It's just that the things he's thinking about, the things he's trying to do, are a much higher motivation for him. They are *so* real to him, *so* vivid... they loom *so* large, and his energy is immense... And because his ideas are what drive him, he wants the freedom to choose those.

Self-determination is especially important to spirited kids – but in the meantime, it isn't really enough just to know that your child has his own agenda, is it? I mean, how do we get him to cooperate with ours? I'll be talking a lot more about this in this book's next chapters, but for now, I want to emphasize the following:

ASSUMPTION #5: YOU HAVE TO HAVE IT BOTH WAYS: THE MOST EFFECTIVE WAY TO GET KIDS' COOPERATION IS TO A) ESTABLISH YOURSELF AS THE ONE IN CHARGE OF THE FAMILY AND B) RELATE TO YOUR CHILD IN A SPIRIT OF COLLABORATION AND PARTNERSHIP.

What I'm saying here is this: If you want your child to be less oppositional and more cooperative, you need to consistently hold him accountable to listen to you and honor the boundaries you set; and you also need to relate to him the way you might a team member, allowing him to share in the decisions that are important to the family. (These decisions might relate to behavior or family patterns that are a problem to parents, or they might be focused on something more neutral.)

On the one hand, "partnering" with your child makes a lot of sense today. Nowadays, for example, most parents and most parenting experts would agree that an authoritarian, "You do it because I said so" approach is harsh and harmful to our kids. And when you relate to your child in a spirit of collaboration, you're not a drill sergeant or dictator; you're working *with* him. Experts also tell us that when you collaborate with your child, this teaches *him* collaboration.

But for spirited kids, *collaboration is about much more than troubleshooting behavior problems in a positive way or the development of negotiation skills*. Another reason it's so helpful to collaborate with these kids is that – if we do it right – it gives them a clear context and structure for expressing their will and exercising the autonomy and choice that's so important to them. Essentially, collaboration meets kids' very real need for autonomy and control, and when this need for control is met in productive ways, they don't have the same impulse to meet the need in unproductive ways.

I'll be sharing a detailed outline of the kind of collaboration I'm talking about in Chapter 5, but for now, let me be clear: You *do* have to have it both ways. While relating to your child as a fellow team member is important, it is not usually sufficient to change behavior.

Some experts want us to address kids' behavior problems using collaboration alone, but this doesn't really work with kids on the far end of the strong-willed spectrum. For one thing, highly-spirited kids tend not to bother to cooperate if at first you don't hold them accountable to do so. The other thing is that accountability is just – necessary. You can't have meaningful boundaries if you don't have a way to hold your child accountable to honor them, and some boundaries are really important. Moreover, boundaries are not inherently damaging – you are not hurting your child when you hold her accountable to, say, put her shoes on, or limit her screen time, or get to bed by 9:00.

Although the main purpose of this book is not to argue against parental permissiveness, I will be providing a rationale for boundary-setting and accountability here and there – because again, boundaries and accountability are important, but many people confuse these with punishment. Generally speaking, and in the ideal scenario, partnership and accountability happen at the same time: You collaborate and partner with your child and at the same time you require that he listen to you, follow household rules, etc. But because truly effective collaboration can't happen until you've established yourself as the authority in your family, I'm going to talk about the discipline side first. We'll focus on parental authority, boundary-setting, and discipline in the next two chapters.

2

LAYING THE GROUNDWORK: PARENTS, YOU'RE IN CHARGE

"The child supplies the power but the parents have to do the steering."

–Benjamin Spock

When your child was a little baby all she needed from you was nurturing, nurturing, nurturing. And every time she cried, you took care of her. Then your baby turned one and started walking, but she still needed you most of the time. And then – and, looking back, you probably know when this happened – there came a point when your baby became much more independent. She was maybe two or two and a half, and all of a sudden she didn't need you the same way anymore. And now we're in the Terrible Twos, right? It happens for kids almost overnight. But it can take parents years to realize that a transition has happened: *Whereas in your child's infancy your primary role was The Nurturer, now, your child needs you to be The Leader*. It's very important that parents recognize this transition for what it is, because when you respond to a 2- or 3-year-old as 100% nurturer you can't provide the leadership that enables her to receive the things you need to teach her.

This point is very important, so let me emphasize it. You must establish yourself as the leader, as the authority in your family, if your child is going to respect you enough to learn from you and relate to you as a teacher and guide. Now, some of what you'll be teaching her is shared decision-making and collaborative problem-solving. You'll be giving her a voice in family decisions and you'll be teaching her to negotiate and seek what she wants in a way that takes everyone's needs into account. And this is one way you'll be *partnering* with your child. But she wasn't born with this knowledge, and children by definition are at a stage in their development in which they are more self-centered and not yet mature enough to make room for others' point of view. So you must *teach* her partnership, and you can't do an excellent job of that unless you also teach her to relate to you as the authority in your home.

Many parents have a problem with being in charge. This may stem from their personal history: Many of us feel that our parents were overbearing or too harsh, and we don't want to raise our kids the way they raised us. And there are even behavior- and relationship theories out there that say that being in charge is inherently oppressive. You can't get around it, they say: You may have all of the responsibility, but if it's not the kid's way or consensus, you're oppressing your child.

When you really think about it, though, having a parent in charge makes a lot of sense! For one thing, when you have rules (and hold your child accountable to follow them) you equip your child to respond effectively to the limits she'll face when she goes out into the world. If she never learns to take No for an answer, what will she do when her teacher says No? Or, let me put it this way – a lot of the dads I work with like this one: If *he* never learns to take No for an answer, what will he do when the girl he's dating says No? Think about it!

In fact, kids *know* that the parents should be in charge. They know that their parents know more than they do. We can reach the wrong conclusion with strong-willed, spirited kids because these kids have so much energy and so much power and so much intention, and it's part of their temperament to push the limits. Imagine that your home and your yard are surrounded by an invisible boundary, and if you could find the weak spot in that boundary, you'd go through that doorway and you'd find yourself in a whole new, wonderful, exciting, satisfying universe. Well, if you really believed in this doorway, you'd keep looking for it. Maybe not every minute, but you'd continue to explore the possibilities. And this is what it's like for your child.

So you have to be just as diligent as she is. Strong-willed kids push and push and push and push partly because they've learned that their parents are *not* as persistent as they are. So they figure if they push hard enough, they'll win. And sometimes that pushing is a screaming meltdown, or an assertion that you're the worst dad in the world and they hate you. Fair enough – they want it their way – but they still know that you should be in charge! Strong-willed kids are emotionally intense and they get really mad when they feel frustrated. The frustration, the anger, the accusations do not in and of themselves indicate that you are oppressing your kids – nor do they mean that your kids *feel* oppressed.

Kids do not feel abused when their parents are in charge, and in fact, kids *want* their parents to be in charge. I know from extensive experience that kids feel more secure when parents are in charge and the boundaries are consistent. I compare this kind of parental leadership to the walls of a house: The parents provide the strong walls, the strong house, and when the kid slams into a wall, the wall doesn't say, Hey, quit running into me, what's the matter with you, why can't you look where you're going? No, the wall doesn't say anything; it just holds that place so the child knows to stop going that way. On the other hand, if the walls were made of Play-Doh, or, say, cardboard – it wouldn't feel secure. The house would not be strong. Anyone could knock the walls down, and no one would feel safe.

My partner and ghostwriter challenges me on this Wall analogy. Handy comparison, she says, But how do we know it's true? Do kids really feel "safer" when their parents are in charge? Yes, they do. I've seen so many kids as a teacher and family coach – even teenagers, when they get this strong boundary-setting from their parents, it's almost as if they can relax into that. You can see it in their faces – they're more relaxed and their expressions are less – confrontational.

And this relaxation connects to the dynamic I described earlier: If strong-willed kids know that there can be a battle of the wills, they'll fight. Conversely, if they've learned that resistance is futile, they can use their incredible energy for something besides fighting. Conflict is stressful! When my parents get really consistent at holding kids accountable to honor the boundaries, kids can relax and they start to relate to the parents as a resource instead of someone they have to challenge. Without fail my parents tell me that their kids just "seem happier."

As I wrap up this section I want to make one more comparison related to the idea that having a parent in charge makes sense. Imagine, for a moment, a family of tigers. When the mama tiger has kittens, she tells the babies where to go and what to do. And when the kittens grow up and no longer need the mama tiger's leadership, they go off on their own. A human has a much longer childhood, but like the tiger, she needs leadership throughout that childhood. A 3-year-old needs a different kind of leadership than the 13-year-old, of course. But if the person never had a leader when they were three, they're going to have a very difficult time relating to a leader as a teenager. I'll share some things that will help you become a more effective leader in the next sections.

Being in charge, Step 1: What are your rules?

The first thing you need to do to establish or strengthen your role as the leader of your family is simply to get very clear about what the family's rules are.

Families have lots of rules. For example, everyone has chores. (I hope your kids have chores. If they don't, give them chores!) There's a bedtime routine everybody follows; everybody has to come to the table to have dinner; the shoes go on the shelf by the front door... Your family has some structure in the way it operates, some agreed-upon rules for "the way we do things around here." And the clearer you and your co-parent are about the rules, the easier it will be for you to get the kids to follow them.

So how do you determine the rules? Typically this isn't a formal meeting with your co-parent. Sometimes it's just "It's OK if they jump on the couch, isn't it?" "Yeah, whatever, the couch is a hundred years old, I don't care."

Still, the rule has been determined: It's OK to jump on the couch. And it's important to be clear about the rules you have in your family.

And it's also really, really important to be clear about what a rule actually is. According to one dictionary definition, a rule is "one of a set of explicit or understood regulations or principles governing conduct within a particular activity or sphere." A rule is a set of *regulations* that *govern* conduct. In other words, a rule is not a *suggestion*, nor is it a *description of your preferences*, nor is it a *reminder of your preferences*.

Family rules are often stated in terms of requests or directives, and a rule about cleaning up after oneself might be indicated by a request such as "Please clean up the mess you made in the kitchen." Suggestions and preferences, on the other hand, come across in statements such as:

- "Amy, why don't you clean up the mess you made in the kitchen," or
- "Amy, I'd really like it if you'd clean up the mess you made in the kitchen," or
- "Amy, you know I hate it when you leave a mess in the kitchen!"

If you want your strong-willed kid to behave in a certain way, you need rules and clear directives related to that behavior. On the other hand, as you know, rules need not be punitive or shaming. It's not, "Clean up the mess you made in the kitchen! You know we all live here! Everybody has to pull their weight. I'm not cleaning it all myself!" It's simply, "Please clean up the mess you made in the kitchen." Because the rules, and your authority as parent-leader, are about much more than getting your child to think about the needs of others. Remember, you are teaching and developing and thus empowering your child to thrive!

Ultimately, then, your rules and boundaries develop self-discipline, self-regulation, the ability to delay gratification... crucial skills and attitudes that will enable her to get more of what *she* wants. So deliver the rules and directives in a non-punitive, non-shaming, neutral tone. And make sure you include "listening" as one of your family's rules.

RULES AND BOUNDARIES ARE NOT SUGGESTIONS OR PREFERENCES

Take the time to notice: When you ask your child to do something, are you actually asking her to do it? Or are you suggesting that she do it? Or are you telling her what you'd like or what you wish?

BEING IN CHARGE, STEP 2: "LISTENING" SHOULD BE A FAMILY RULE

I think it's really important that parents include "listening" as one of their family rules. Most of the parents I work with tell me that their child does not listen, and in my experience, most parents think their kids *should* listen. So am I stating the obvious? If you want your kid to listen, why am I telling you to include listening in your rulebook?

Well, I think parents are of two minds about listening. They know kids should listen. And they may be willing to agree on specific family rules, like, Bedtime is at 8:00. Nevertheless, despite the rule, when it comes time to hold that boundary they find themselves in a lengthy communication dance: Bedtime is at 8, OK:

You: "Billy, it's time for bed."

Billy: "OK, just let me finish this show," or "No, I don't want to go to bed."

You: "Billy, it's time for *bed*. It's 8:00!"

Billy: "OK, I'm going!" [Billy continues to watch TV.]

You: "Dammit, Billy, it's time for bed!! Now!!"

So there are rules, but we find ourselves repeating and repeating and repeating the directive to follow the rules. Or, what if you're just making a request that has nothing to do with an established rule? "Billy, please stop teasing your sister." Or, "Billy, would you please clear the table – our family coach will be here in ten minutes." Parents are of two minds about listening. They believe kids should listen, but if kids don't, parents just repeat themselves. Or they can make excuses. "Oh, she's not feeling well today." I hear that one a lot!

But I think parents should hold kids accountable to listen. Moreover, I define listening as *responding to a directive the first time the directive is given*. In other words *even if your child eventually does the thing*, it isn't listening if you have to keep repeating yourself, or if you have to yell or threaten.

Now, I know some parents think this hard line is arrogant and harsh: "Do it because I say so." But – remember your teacher's mindset – our intention is not to be harsh. Instead, we're simply being very clear about establishing ourselves as the leaders in our family. Because what's actually happening when your child is *not* listening? When he is not listening, he's essentially saying No to you. No, I'm not going to do that. He may *say* No, or he may say Yes I will at some point in the future. But when he is not in fact doing what you've asked him to do, what he usually means is *No, not until I know you really mean it*.

And if you're serious about being the authority in your home, you're not going to allow the refusal to follow your directives as a viable option. Think of the basketball coach. You may find it distasteful to compare your family to a sports team, but just consider a sports context for a minute, because it gives us a solid perspective on what it means to be an authority. With the basketball team, the coach says how it will go, and things are set up in such a way that just saying No – or often not *saying* No but actually *intending* No – is never OK. Your child needs to listen to you!

On the other hand, he doesn't have to agree – and in fact, he should be encouraged to speak his mind (in a way that's respectful, of course). As I suggested earlier, you parent most effectively when you *partner* with your child, honoring his voice, honoring his perspective, and showing him how to pursue what he wants through negotiation and compromise. But negotiation is very different from "not listening." And in the most effective parent-child partnerships – because the parent is still the one with the responsibility, the one who knows more and is developmentally more able to make rational decisions – the child is *not* a peer with 50% of the decision-making power. The parent is still the parent, and the main way parents establish themselves as leaders is to require their kids to listen.

How MANY TIMES DO YOU WANT TO SAY IT?

"How many times do I have to say it?" This is actually a question kids can answer. Sometimes I'll hear a mom ask her child this question. Of course, she's expressing frustration – she's not really expecting an answer – so then I'll ask the child, Well, how many times does she have to tell you? And they'll give me a number. They know exactly how many times you say it before they have to do it.

So how many times do you *want* to say it? Most experts tell us to give directives in a calm, neutral tone, and I'm going to be saying that too – and honestly, one reason I have parents teach their kids to listen the first time is because it's a whole lot easier to be calm when you only have to say it once. You can teach your child to respond the first time, or you can teach her that she doesn't have to listen until the tenth time and you're screaming and your cortisol levels have skyrocketed. I have some parents who would rather have the child respond the third time. OK, fine. But if she responds sooner vs. later, this means a lot less stress, frustration, and wasted time for you – and for her.

And how do you get your child to listen to you the first time or the third time? You hold her accountable to do so. We'll talk more about accountability in the next section.

BEING IN CHARGE, STEP 3: HOLD YOUR CHILD ACCOUNTABLE

If you agree that parents should have rules, and you're reading this book because your strong-willed child doesn't follow the rules, an important first step is to get very clear about what your rules are. But it's not enough to just *have* a rule, right?

So once you know what your rules are, you need to hold your child accountable to follow them. And accountability means consequences. Accountability means *answerability*. Accountability is not positive reinforcement. It is not the same thing as explaining the reason for ("talking about") a rule, or reminding the child to follow the rule, or urging the child to follow the rule. Accountability requires a person to answer for his actions, and this in turn implies a consequence if those actions are objectionable.

On the other hand, given that many parents place a very high value on "positive" discipline nowadays, we probably need to address this question: Why do we need consequences? We shouldn't punish our kids; the goal should be simply to teach the desired behavior. So why isn't explaining the reason for the behavior or rewarding a desired behavior enough?

ACCOUNTABILITY IS NOT ABUSE

I'll be talking about "negative" vs. "positive" consequences in the next chapter, but I think the first, most important answer to these questions is this: Accountability is not punishment. Consequences are not punishment. The parenting pendulum has swung very far away from consequences and really holding kids accountable to listen because parents don't want to be punitive tyrants. But consequences and punishment are actually separate things.

So here's another place where mindset is really important: Remember, accountability is simply *answerability*. Consequences are simply a result that follows from a behavior or set of behaviors. In this context, of course, we are talking about the results humans impose as opposed to, say, the results of gravity. So if I drop and break that beautiful ceramic tile I see in the gift shop, I have to pay for it. I have a real responsibility to that shop owner; I can't just do what I please and if my actions result in consequences that are negative for her, I'll just leave her to deal with it.

We *want* our kids to develop a sense of responsibility, a sense that we have to answer for our behavior and we can't just do whatever we want. And answering for our behavior is more than just *knowing* that something wasn't nice. It's not, OK, I'll *talk* to her about it, because then she'll *know* it. Rebecah, you shouldn't be so careless with that tile. How would you feel if someone broke something of yours?

Kids understand accountability. Let me give you an example: For several years now I've been working with a child whose family has had a difficult time setting boundaries with her. Now, though, Julie is nine, her behavior is increasingly more difficult to manage, and her mom is now open to consequences.

Recently Julie took her mom's house keys and hid them for three days. Mom didn't know that Julie had taken them – she just thought she had left them somewhere, and this was a big worry for her. And when we learned that Julie had hidden them – one day she just pulled them from the hiding place and returned them – I said to Julie, "Well, what consequence do you think we should have for that?" Remember, consequences are a very new thing in this household, and Julie doesn't like them at all. But she answered, "I should probably not get to watch TV 'til Sunday." Because Julie *knows* that she needs to be held accountable. Consequences being new to her, at this point she's resisting them as a matter of course, but when I asked her how she should answer for hiding the keys she did not say, Oh, I shouldn't have to do anything. I should just get to do whatever I want. Because she has an intuitive sense that consequences are appropriate. "Yeah, I deserve to answer for creating that chaos in my home."

Accountability is not punishment, and along the same lines, I really want to reassure those of you who fear that accountability and consequences might hurt your child or break his spirit. They most definitely will not, if stay in your role as leader and teacher. And this is *especially* true for spirited kids. I've experienced this over and over in my work with them. These kids love intensity – not only in themselves, but in others. They can handle strength. They respect *your* strong will and your strength. This doesn't mean they won't push back – they will! And I'm not saying that it's OK to hurt them because they can handle it. I'm simply saying that spirited kids have some serious spirit, and rules and consequences for breaking the rules do not hurt them, especially if you deliver these, not as policeman or as offended, angry parent, but as teacher, mentor, and coach.

SPIRITED KIDS CAN HANDLE IT

One time I was working with a child in her home because her mom needed me to model the kind of boundary-setting we had been talking about in my office. (Mom had tried on her own to implement what I had taught her, but the technique wasn't working because she had been reluctant to really follow through.) I'll be describing the way in which I held this girl accountable in Chapter 3, but the point of this story is that the boundary-setting did not hurt this child – although she did get angry, and she did push back!

The problem was that she wouldn't listen, and as I was engaged in the process of holding her accountable to listen, she hid in her closet and yelled and yelled: "I hate you!" "I want you out of this house!" "I want you out of this world, and out of Berkeley!" And then, after I had consistently applied the consequence and applied the consequence and applied the consequence (this took about 20 minutes), she got out of the closet, did what she had been asked to do, and calmly went about her evening as if the incident had never happened. Spirited kids can handle strength, and they respect *your* strong will and your strength. Don't be afraid to hold them accountable – it isn't going to hurt them!

Remember, rules and limits give us the real-world practice we need to develop the self-discipline we need to do the difficult things we'd rather not do. And the ability to do the hard things, to follow a plan and not just act on an impulse, can lead a child to greatness. So when you hold your child accountable, first, check your mindset. Provide accountability with the intention to equip and empower your child, and you won't be coming from a place of anger and retaliation. I share one of the most effective tools for holding kids accountable in the next chapter.

3

LAYING THE GROUNDWORK:
ACCOUNTABILITY MEANS
CONSEQUENCES

"I think of discipline as the continual everyday process of
helping a child learn self-discipline."

–Mr. Rogers

In the last chapter I emphasized the need for you, as the
parent, to establish yourself as the leader in your family.
And of course being a leader is more than just, "Oh, yeah,
of course I'm in charge – I'm the adult." Being a leader
is more than just having all of the responsibility; and we
don't just say that we're in charge because it would be very
uncomfortable to look more closely and admit to ourselves
that our child is often in charge. In fact, you are *not* a leader
if your lead is not *followed* – you're not a leader if your child
does not respect your authority as the parent.

Earlier I said that if your child does not follow you, if she insists on her own way instead, then you should hold her accountable for that – and accountability means consequences – but consequences do not have to mean punishment; they can mean, simply, education. *It all hinges on your mindset and your intention.* Remember, not only are you not intending to punish your child; ultimately you're not even intending to stop "bad" behavior: Your intention is mainly to teach, equip, and empower. But you can't actually do a good job of that unless you're seen as an authority.

Some parenting experts will consider the consequence I'm about to share with you to be negative. This is because the consequence *is* in fact uncomfortable for the child. Basically, the consequence is a parental response that says "I'm in charge, and when you break a rule or choose not to listen, I'm not going to just let that go. Nor am I going to engage with whatever verbal resistance you may offer. Instead, when you choose not to listen, I'll hold you accountable, which means you'll pay a price. *On the other hand, I do want to work with you to give you what you want.*"

Isn't this awesome! *The consequence I'll be describing is actually intended to lead kids to develop appropriate ways of getting what they want, so they no longer need to fight you.* We'll talk more about these appropriate alternatives later. For now, my point is that the consequence *is* uncomfortable for the child, in part because you want to motivate her to listen, but also because you want to *develop her ability to get what she wants* in ways that work for everyone.

Wait a minute, you may be asking. Why the heck do we need a negative consequence to teach kids to listen and cooperate? There are so many other ways to discipline.

There are sticker charts – you could give young Andrew a reward for good behavior. Or there are "natural" consequences – for example, Amy refuses to wear her coat and experiences discomfort when she gets cold. Or you could just explain the importance of the rule, and provide verbal instruction in behaviors that are more desirable: "Jimmy, it's really important that we don't hit. You *hurt* people when you hit them. Use your words instead!"

Well, you're right. These more "positive" techniques *do* work for a lot of kids. And if that works for your kid, then you're probably reading the wrong book. Because, remember, I'm talking to parents of *spirited* kids – those kids who run out of natural consequences by 7:45 a.m. Or, when you ask them, would you like the red shirt or the blue shirt, they insist on *your* shirt, or their pajamas, or no shirt at all...

Many or most of today's discipline techniques don't work with spirited kids – or if they do work, they work only for a short time – because, as I mentioned earlier, a) spirited kids are energetic, intelligent and imaginative enough that their own plans are incredibly vivid and enticing; b) these kids are not on the high end of the people-pleaser spectrum; they do not have an especially high need for approval; and c) these kids have a high need for autonomy and control.

To put it another way, today's consequences don't work with spirited kids because essentially these strategies ask the child to cooperate in exchange for something that, to them, is superficial or inconsequential. Spirited kids want a lot more than a sticker on the chart. Their strong will and low inclination to please, relative to other kids – along with their place in the course of human development – means they are not highly motivated by your explanations or talks. Get ready for bed and then *go* to bed? Most of the time the spirited child is willing to give up the sticker in exchange for control over their evening – along with a chance to prove their autonomy by making a significant impact on the bedtime routine.

A while ago, a parent inquiring about my services wrote in an email, "We have tried positive discipline, but it has just seemed to spoil the kids. They don't seem to appreciate positive rewards." But when the parents I work with hold their child accountable with a consequence that actually positions the parents as in charge, they see a significant decrease in the problem behavior. I *do* work with a lot of parents who at first resist the idea of a negative consequence. But I show them how the consequence is an empowering education vs. punishment – *and I show them how we'll also be using tools that give the child a serious voice and a profound sense of control* (see Chapter 5) – and, because the parents are so stressed out, they give my technique a try. "What technique is that," you ask? I'll give you an overview, below.

THE TAKE-AWAY

In my experience one of the most effective tools there is to hold kids accountable to listen and follow the rules is a tool I call the Take-Away. In the sections below I'm going to describe the technique; tell you how to implement it; tell you what *not* to do as you use this tool; remind you why it works; and show you how to respond to some of the main obstacles kids will throw at you when you're first getting started. As you read, though, please keep in mind that it's not possible for me to give you a complete picture in a few pages or a chapter. So at the end of this chapter I'll show you where to go for more information that will allow you to really use this tool in a way that's effective and empowering.

Essentially, the Take-Away works like this: When you give a directive and your child doesn't listen, you take toys or other things – things he knows are his – until he decides to listen. Then, a few days later, you give the things back. That's it. It's simple, really.

First, give your kids a heads-up: "OK, from now on we're going to do things a little differently. Starting tomorrow, from now on, when I tell you to do something, you need to do it. And if you don't do it when I tell you to, I'm going to take one of your things away." Then, the next day, when Tommy doesn't do what you told him to do (or when he doesn't stop doing what you told him to stop), you say, for example: "Tommy, I see that you are not clearing the table. I'm going to take one of your things away." And then simply take that thing, put it some place where he can't get to it, tell him again to clear the table, and if he doesn't clear the table at that point: "You are still not clearing the table." And then take something else.

The Take-Away works with kids as young as two or as old as 18. Your child's age doesn't really impact *how* you use this tool, though age is a factor when it comes to introducing the concept and returning the things you've taken. A 2- or 3-year-old will need a few reminders per day over the course of two or three days: "You are not putting your shoes away. I'm taking a toy. You'll get your toys back on Wednesday." Four- and 5-year-olds can use reminders for one day. And with children six or older, just introduce the concept – they don't need reminders.

If you both implement the Take-Away and create a collaborative relationship with your child when he's younger, you'll find that after a while you won't need the Take-Away very often. But it's always good to have this tool "in your back pocket" in situations that require immediate, simple consequences.

How to do it

Now, here are a few details to keep in mind as you use the Take-Away – some of these are key, and others will just make the process easier for you. We'll start with the things you should *do*:

--Take the little things. A marble. A sock. A book. A crayon. As you can see, by *things*, I mean something *concrete*. For example, things are not future enjoyable events like the birthday party on Saturday. And I'm going to say this again, because it's key: Take mainly *little* things. A Lego. A toy truck. A pen. Another sock. I'll talk more about this in a minute, but for now, believe me – I've learned through vast experience that taking little things is actually more effective than taking big things. *This also makes the Take-Away easier for you to implement, which in turn helps you to be consistent.*

--Keep it simple. You'll see more of what I mean when you read what *not* to do. For now, re-read my example above and notice how simple it is. You give the directive, he doesn't listen, you acknowledge that he's not listening and you state that because of this you'll take a toy, and you take a toy. And you repeat this process until he listens. It's simple!

--Along these same lines, use a neutral tone. Remember, this is not punishment. You are not judging him, you're not mad at him (if you *are* mad, remind yourself that accountability is intended only to empower him and try not to show it). You're simply taking charge of the situation, and to maintain your role as leader you're showing him that if he chooses not to listen, there will be a consequence. We want the consequence to be simply an emotionally neutral but undesirable result that follows a choice not to listen. This keeps punishment and anger out of it; it means you're not fighting with him; and a neutral tone also enhances his view of you as a leader – you're in control of your emotions.

--When you take things, do it so that he sees it or hears it. For one thing, he needs to experience this consequence in a vivid way – you aren't *threatening* to take something in the future; you're actually taking it. And for parents who are first learning this process, it really helps if he sees you. This is because, again, we want a neutral tone – but in the beginning it's hard to actually *be* neutral – and you won't have to repeat "I'm taking another toy" if he can just see you taking it. *I* can say, "You're still not listening – I'm taking another toy" 83 times without feeling or sounding frustrated, partly because of my perspective on kids and discipline and partly because I know without any doubt whatsoever that this process works. But parents who are new at this get frustrated when they have to keep taking things away, and it can be easier for them to appear neutral if they don't have to talk!

--When your child decides he's had enough of your taking things and he does what you want him to do, say, "Thank you." That's all you have to say. Just, "Thank you."

--Determine which day of the week you'll give the toys back. This keeps things simple and neutral: In response to the question, "Will I get my truck back?" you won't be as tempted to respond with anger or punishment. "We'll see – I'm really tired of having to tell you to hang up your backpack..." No, there's a system. "I'll give you your things back on Wednesday."

And when you return your child's things, keep it simple: Say only, "Here are your things." Do not add to this message. Say only, "Here are your things." Oh, and say this in a neutral tone.

And later – only after your child is familiar with the process – have him do something to *earn* the things you took. At first we want to return things without his having to earn them because this helps him to know, yes, I *will* get my things back. But later it's best if, to get things returned, he does something that contributes to the family in a concrete way. He can do one of your chores (but he needs to do it in a way that actually relieves you of that job). He can repair something in the house that's broken, do extra yard work, care for a younger sibling... Anything that contributes to the household – and when you're ready for it, decide what this will be in a Family Meeting (see Chapter 5). This way you and he will make the decision together.

WHAT NOT TO DO

Now let's talk about some things that should *not* be included in the Take-Away:

--Don't take away events, privileges like TV, or special toys like the teddy bear she sleeps with at night. A lot of parents have a lot of trouble with this piece, but take my word for it, the Take-Away is not about taking the "big," special things that are important to her. Never take away the teddy bear that comforts and grounds her. Don't take away the big thing you know she's looking forward to: "Well, she kicked that kid at school and she doesn't deserve to go to that birthday party."

But the Take-Away is not about "deserving" or not deserving. *And more important, the impact you are making is not due to the pain she might experience when you take something really important.* Yes, that pain *would* have an impact, but with really strong-willed kids, *not only are there not enough big things to take away, when you take away the little things – if you are consistent – this is impact enough.* The Take-Away works for the same reason a rock sitting under a dripping fountain will eventually turn into a bowl: *This technique is not about pain, it's about consistent, non-punitive responses that show her you mean what you say and whenever she doesn't listen, you'll hold her accountable.* I'll say it again: Taking big things doesn't work because there aren't enough of them and taking little things consistently has a huge impact on someone with a high need for control. Because these kids don't want you taking *anything* – because this puts *you* in control. Taking the little things is all the consequence you need.

--Don't repeat yourself, give warnings, or make threats. This isn't, "Julie, clear the table." "Julie, I *said*, Clear the table." "Julie, if you don't clear the table I'm going to take a toy." "*Julie...*" No! For one thing, those warnings teach her that she doesn't have to listen the first time because you'll be repeating yourself a few more times before you actually do anything. And more important, *you lose a huge opportunity to develop and teach your child when you treat this consequence as something you have to help her avoid.* When you're in the moment like this – when you've given a directive and she isn't listening – *it's actually less important that she do the specific thing you've asked her to do and more important that you use this time for what it is – an opportunity to teach her to listen.* Because when you set limits and she is held accountable to listen, this positions you as the leader and, equally as important, it gives her the experiences she needs to develop self-discipline and self-control. The Take-Away will teach her and develop her and ultimately empower her. Use it for what it is – a teaching tool. You don't have to protect her from it.

--Don't engage in arguments or Q&As. Kids are masters at engaging adults in conversations as a way to avoid doing what the grownup told them to do. "Why do I have to put my shoes away? Daddy didn't put his shoes away." Good point, but in fact this is irrelevant. "How come I have to put my shoes away? I went over to my friend's house and they never have to put their shoes away." OK, now with this one I really want to say "Well, you don't live at your friend's house; you live with me." But I'm not going to say anything, because my kid's main intention is to avoid doing what I've asked her to do, and so I'm going to maintain my simple boundary: I asked you to put your shoes away. When you don't listen, I take one of your things. *This* is what should happen when kids don't listen – the result should never be a conversation. Like so many of us, most kids enjoy verbal expression. Engaging you is something they enjoy – and when you're dealing with a high-energy person who isn't overly concerned about your approval, engaging you is fun even when you're yelling!

So don't answer the Why? or the But... or the It's not fair... And don't answer their intellectual curiosity, either – not right away, anyway. "Julie, put your shoes away." "Mom, how do you make shoes?" Kids love to ask these questions because they know we love how smart they are. They love it that we love it that they want to know everything. And they know that we want to tell them everything. "Are these shoes made of rubber or is rubber going extinct?" They know you love it when they use big words. But I'm not going to say anything, and if Julie doesn't put her shoes away, I'll take a toy.

But then, after she does put her shoes away, I remember that she wanted to know how shoes are made, so I'm going to ask, "Do you still want to know how shoes are made? Because we can look that up." Now, Julie probably *doesn't* want to know at this point, because her question was mainly an attempt to bypass my directive. But when I follow up with her she's going to know, "Oh,

Mom heard me and she's taking me seriously. But I still have to put my shoes away."

--Don't add to the message: "Julie, please hang up your coat. You *know* you're not supposed to leave it on the table. That table is my office space." Or, "You didn't hang up your coat, so I'm taking your book. You *know* that when you don't listen, I take one of your things. You need to listen to me when I tell you something. I don't know how many times I have to explain this to you." No! The message should simply be, "You didn't do what I told you to do, so I'm going to take your [some small thing]." Remember, keep it simple. When you give the directive, don't explain it – she already knows why you want her to do it because you've already told her 100 times. And don't remind her how the Take-Away works, either.

I'm not trying to turn you into a drill sergeant, here. It's just that with the Take-Away, less really is more. When you keep it simple the lesson is clearer and the exchange is more neutral than it is when you add to it. *Your explanations are not where the learning occurs.* The learning happens as a result of the consequence itself – your taking the thing very soon after she chooses not to follow you. So don't detract from the lesson with superfluous messaging.

And this same point holds when you return her things to her. Remember what the message should be? "Here's your things." Not, "Here's your things. I had to take *this* one because you didn't hang up your coat. I took *this* one because you didn't get ready for bed when I asked you to. I took *this* because you called the dog a bad name. Geez, I sure hope you'll do better this week!"

No. When you return her things, *think of it as a clean slate*. Whether during the Take-Away itself or when you're returning her things a week later, there's nowhere in the process where we want to recite that list of things she's always doing wrong. Don't complain to her about what she did wrong and how difficult she is, ever, ever, ever again. Keep all disapproval out of it. Remember, the lesson is not, make her feel guilty and then she'll change her ways – the lesson is simply, When you don't listen, here's a consequence. So stop telling her what she's done wrong and instead give her a list of all the things she does right, and if she's only done one thing right then tell her about it ten times. Because the judgment only causes harm. But your telling her what she did right encourages her and shows her that you're on her side.

CONSISTENCY: HERE'S A WAY TO MAKE THAT EASIER...

So now I've given you a brief overview of what the Take-Away is and how to use it. So let's talk for a minute about consistency. Consistency is one of the staples of parenting books: If you're going to hold a child accountable to follow a rule, you have to be consistent. You have to consistently hold him accountable.

It *is* important to be consistent. And of course the more consistent you are about holding your child to specific rules, the better. If you think about it, if you really want your child to follow your lead, to follow the rules, it's better not to have a rule than to have the rule and let your child break it. Because when you let your child break the rule you're essentially telling him that he doesn't have to follow it. So if it's really difficult for you to be consistent about a rule then you should let that rule go.

But also, I want you to shift your thinking on consistency a little, to make things easier for you. Because one reason consistency is so difficult is that parents are overworked and overwhelmed, and it's really, really hard to focus on consistent discipline when the car just broke down and you're late for work and you ran out of coffee... But if you shift from thinking in terms of all the different rules you have and think instead, "When I say it, you need to listen," *listening* can become the place where you're always consistent, *and this focus also provides a flexibility that doesn't undermine your authority*. Because when you aren't giving a directive, he doesn't say No, and when he doesn't say No, you don't need to hold him accountable.

It's true that we're always going to want the kids to hang their coats up and go to bed on time. And when they don't hang up their coat, ask them to do it. But when circumstances make it difficult for you to provide real leadership in the face of their No, don't ask, and then you won't get the No. A focus on listening doesn't mean there are no rules about coats or bedtime; but when the rules are incorporated within the main rule – listening – this puts you in a position where, if you choose to let bedtime-at-8:00 go for the night, you're still behaving like the one in charge.

WAIT A MINUTE. IS THE TAKE-AWAY *REALLY* A GOOD IDEA?

Now that I've talked about consequences and the Take-Away in some detail, you probably have a clearer idea of how and why the Take-Away works. Still, there is so much in our culture today that makes it difficult for parents to see consequences as anything but punishment. Perhaps on the one hand consequences make some sense. On the other hand – taking her toys away!! How is that not punitive? Again, though, consequences that cause discomfort are not negative or punitive *if you use them with a genuine, clear intention to develop (and ultimately empower) your child*. If you use it as I've shown you here, the Take-Away is a non-punitive discipline technique that's especially appropriate for strong-willed, spirited kids because

--If you do it right, **it establishes you as the one in charge of the household.** Now, with kids who really want to please you or kids who are more cooperative by nature you may not actually need to assert yourself as the one in charge. But with a strong-willed or oppositional kid, if you're not in charge, she will be. And she shouldn't be, because she doesn't yet have the knowledge, experience, and maturity she needs to make great decisions.

--**It establishes you as the leader,** and your child needs to see you as a leader if she's going to follow you, learn from you, and really receive everything you want to teach her.

--**It gives kids the concrete, real-world experiences that enable them to develop self-control and self-discipline.** Humans learn to delay gratification, to impose limits on themselves, not through "explanations" or "talks," but through experience. When a child has rules she has to follow, she has tangible experience with limits and requirements that in turn give her experience and practice in things like following a schedule or keeping the living environment clean or negotiating instead of hitting.

--It provides the foundation that **enables her to learn a more productive way to get what she wants.** Again, the Take-Away is intended to work in conjunction with other tools that give your child the appropriate venue for expressing her desires and exerting her will. Ideally you and your child would resolve disagreements using negotiation and collaborative problem-solving, and I'll be showing you how to do that. But why would an oppositional child collaborate with you if she doesn't even have to listen to you – if she's already running the show?

--Finally, although I've focused on the Take-Away as a tool that establishes you as the one in charge, it's also helpful to remember that *the Take-Away also puts the kids in charge.* Because the Take-Away is simply a consequence, and it's not force and it's not highly aversive (say, in the way corporal punishment could be), the choice kids make is very real: I can listen and do this thing I don't want to do, or I can lose a toy for a week. There's no intimidation or duress at play here.

When I'm describing the Take-Away to a family one of the questions I ask the kids is, "Who's in control of how many toys get taken?" And at first they pout because they think I'm going to lecture them, and they say, "My mom and my dad." And I say, "No, you are. You are in control of how many toys get taken away because you are in control of whether you listen or not." And then as I'm continuing to work with the family I'll ask the kids, "What did you choose this week? How many toys did you choose to have taken away?" And this kind of conversation and re-frame helps the kids see that this really is a choice – *and in turn this actually honors their need for control.*

BUT WHAT IF THEY...

When I told you how to implement the Take-Away I said that the process is actually pretty simple: If they don't listen you take something away, and you keep taking things until they listen. On the other hand, there are a few typical responses kids bring that are really challenging for parents, that make it difficult for parents to see the process through.

One big challenge kids present in response to the Take-Away is to tell you that they don't care. "You didn't do this, so I'm taking a toy." "Go ahead, I don't care." Or, some kids will start throwing toys at you: "Here, take these too. Take all of them; take them all!" And this drives parents crazy because they're supposed to care, right? They're supposed to say, "No, please, no, don't take my toy, I'll be a good boy now!" Don't let the "I don't care" throw you. Just keep taking toys until they listen. If they give you toys to take away, you can choose: Take those toys or take something else. It's up to you – you're the one in charge.

Remember, these are kids who have a high need for control. And if they really didn't care, they *would* be in control – and this connects to my point that you should maintain an even, neutral tone, right? Because if you are not emotionally rattled, you are in control. And kids will try to assure you that they are a rock, and you are having no impact on them whatsoever, simply as a means of regaining control.

But if you see this process through, I promise, you *will* get results. Because sooner or later, kids do care. When they see that you mean it, and you will keep taking things and keep taking things and keep taking things, they care! I've never once seen the Take-Away fail when it's used as I describe it here. And the record, see if you can beat it, and if you can, send me an e-mail – the record is 105 toys taken away in one session. And after that 105th toy the child got up; did what her mom asked her to do (Mom had asked her to put her pajamas on); and then sat on Mom's lap for story time as if nothing had ever happened.

The other big challenge for parents happens when the child responds with physical aggression. What if your child hits you, or kicks you – or tries to grab the toys away from you? In this case you should disengage from him, because disengaging is one of the best ways to teach kids that it's not OK to use violence. To do this you either remove yourself from the environment or you put the child in a separate room. *How* you disengage depends on how big they are, how strong you are, if they're going to tear the house apart, etc., but the important thing is to disengage so that they can't continue to kick or hit or grab. And when they're calm enough to make that choice to keep their bodies to themselves, you need to make the request again: "Please put your shoes on."

(Again, though, keep it simple. You're not going to give a stern, angry command because this time it was over the line and by golly he should never have hit you. And you're not going to say, "Now, was that so hard?" when he finally does the thing. Because for him, given his developmental stage and his intense energy and will and drive and imagination and his need for control and he was focused on this whole other thing or maybe he just really needed a break and you come in with this puny idea of Put your shoes on – Yeah, it *was* hard for him to transition from his thing to your thing. And you're going to work with him and partner with him and he'll learn how to transition more easily but right now he just needs to transition. And when you hold him accountable without judging or reacting emotionally he learns to know and accept himself and he learns to trust and cooperate with you.)

OK, I TRIED IT BUT WHAT ABOUT...

As I said in the beginning of this section, it's not possible for me to describe the Take-Away in complete detail in a few pages. If you'd like to get answers to some of the most frequently-asked questions about the Take-Away, you can access that on my website (http://witsendparenting.com/ttainfo). And better yet, if you'd like me to coach you through this process, I'm happy to work with you. Go here (http://witsendparenting.com/ttacourse) to learn more about a program that will help you to use this tool effectively and in a way that's right for your child.

4

Partnering With Your Spirited Child, Part I: Mindset

"Don't let yourself become so concerned with raising a good kid that you forget you already have one."

–Glennon Melton

At the beginning of this book I said that if you want your child to be less oppositional and more cooperative, you need to consistently hold him accountable to honor the boundaries you set and you also need to *partner* with him, for example, by inviting him to share in decisions about what's expected of him. We talked about parental authority and discipline in Chapters 2 and 3. Now I want to share perspectives and tools that will help you to create and/or strengthen your ability to relate to your child as a partner and fellow team member.

Before I do that, though, I want to point out that my take on this kind of collaborative relationship is a little different from that of a lot of other behavior experts. Most behavior experts (and parents) value collaboration with kids mainly because this represents a "positive" alternative to the "old-school," authoritarian, top-down parenting so many of us experienced when we were kids. Experts also tell us that when you collaborate with your child, you're teaching *him* collaboration, negotiation, consensus – which means your child is developing the skills he needs to get what he wants in appropriate ways. And some experts even believe that collaboration should *replace* accountability entirely.

I agree that kids may be more willing to cooperate with adults who show them that they're on their side and respect their point of view. And I think it's important to pay a lot of attention to developing spirited kids' ability to collaborate and negotiate, precisely because these kids' temperaments predispose them to be more intensely focused on their own goals.

But another reason I believe it's essential to create collaborative partnerships with spirited kids is because this partnership addresses (and satisfies) their need for autonomy and control. It's true that earlier in this book I said that parents – not kids – should be in charge: As you know if you've read the first part of this book, I am not one of those experts who feel that collaborative problem-solving eliminates the need for accountability! On the other hand, it's natural for humans to value control, and spirited kids value it more than most. Spirited kids actually *need* to exert their will; therefore, they need parents to *share* the control that comes with their position as the family's leaders. And one excellent way to share control with kids is to relate to them in a spirit of partnership and collaboration.

The rest of this book will show you how you can create a cooperative, collaborative partnership with your child. One of the best tools for teaching and facilitating cooperation is my Failproof Family Meeting, and I'll be talking about that in detail. Again, though, effective parenting is more than just techniques; your mindset or perspective plays an equally important role in your ability to work with your child in a way that both supports him and encourages him to respond to you. I share two really helpful parenting perspectives in the next sections.

KEY PERSPECTIVE #1: THERE'S NOTHING WRONG WITH YOUR KID!

I am very grateful for my ability to see kids' problem behaviors in a positive light. And the parents I work with feel better about their kids when they learn to see their kids in this light. When parents see their child's bad behavior as a strength – or as a potential strength – the behavior is no longer a problem; instead, it's an opportunity. Parents' frustration levels decrease and they're also more able to stay in their role as leaders whose goal is to develop and empower their kids.

There is nothing wrong with your kid.

This is a key point, one I really emphasize, especially with parents who have children who are a little older; maybe eight or nine or ten years old. These kids have been through preschool. They've been through kindergarten, through a couple of grades of middle school. Some of their teachers have been great, some of their teachers have diagnosed them with something the first day they walked into the classroom. And you may be thinking in the back of your mind or the front of your mind that there must be something wrong because her reactions are so severe, her meltdowns are so severe. Her teachers are telling you that she's different from all the other kids. The parents in your babysitting co-op are telling each other that they don't want to watch your kid. A pediatrician or a psychiatrist or a masters-level therapist may have diagnosed your child with ADHD or ODD.

But even though your child is different from many other kids, and even though parenting her has been difficult, and whether or not she has a psychiatric diagnosis – the fact is that for the vast majority of these kids, their behaviors and their personality stem from their natural temperament. Moreover, their behavior is often developmentally appropriate, pointing simply to a need for education and training. Because all kids enter into a developmental stage where they're self-centered, strong-willed, they're more emotional than rational, they may be aggressive... And it's our job to teach them how to deal with those limits that are so frustrating, and how to exert their will in ways that work for everyone. And if the kid didn't get this training? I've worked with older kids who I *know* didn't get the boundary-setting they needed when they were young, and now no regular school will take them. Do these kids have Oppositional-Defiant Disorder – which, like ADHD, is technically a mental illness? No! They simply weren't taught to get along.

Of course, *lots* of experts would agree that bad behavior points to the child's need to learn more appropriate behaviors. And I know I'm not the first person to say that there's nothing wrong with spirited kids – today, many of us normalize the "spirited" personality type. But what a lot of people don't see is that, especially with spirited kids, *the difficult temperament traits are actually the solution.* Let me say that again. Some experts say, Oh, there's nothing wrong with spirited kids – but let me show you how to "tame" that spirit. Others acknowledge that difficult kids have strengths, and tell us we should look for them – even though they (to quote one expert) "may be hard to find." I am not saying, Look for the strengths. I am saying, This kid's problems *are* her strengths.

For example, take someone who's single-minded and stubborn, who won't take No for an answer. Or someone who has five meltdowns a day. Take someone who's hyperactive; someone who's "too sensitive"; or someone with poor impulse control, who may even be aggressive.

Well, single-minded, stubborn, strong-willed people are tenacious and persistent. The child who angers easily may be strong-willed and may also have a low frustration tolerance – which means he has high expectations and is unwilling to "settle." The kid with too much energy can get a lot done, if you channel that energy. And the sensitive kid? He's the one who's *perceptive*. He doesn't cope by dulling or denying his senses, and he's often the "canary in the coal mine" – the person who provides advance notice when something in the environment isn't right. Finally, the kid with poor impulse control can make decisions and act quickly; and the aggressive child is often single-minded and strong-willed.

It *is* hard to deal with a strong-willed person who won't consider you or cooperate with you. It can be hard to deal with someone who has strong emotional reactions. But it's important to slow down and really see the strong will, the intensity and the energy for what it is. These are very real strengths. We want to give our kids the skills and perspective they need to solve their problems appropriately and work with others and not against them, *but it's important to recognize that most of those behaviors and traits we find so challenging are themselves undeveloped strengths.*

A strong-willed, spirited person is someone who won't let any obstacle stand in her way. She can overcome any barrier – and also, she won't be intimidated by other strong personalities. Certainly, these traits will "help her succeed in life." But these traits equip her for much more than the "success" some refer to when they speak of the impor- tance of, say, a good education or a nurturing environment. Should she face an incredibly difficult personal challenge, she'll be able to handle it, because she's unstoppable. And should she choose to take on some of the incredible chal- lenges we face as a global community, she'll be able to do that, too. (Spirited kids, especially, have the will and the perseverance to make big change. One reason I think it's so important to nurture and develop our spirited kids' spirit is because these are the kind of people who will insist on the changes our communities need to survive and thrive.)

I want you to see your child's difficult behavior as an undeveloped strength rather than a problem to be fixed. Because again, not only will this perspective-shift ease your frustration, it will also encourage and support you in teaching, developing, and empowering your child. Let's say your kid is one of those extra fussy kids who has five meltdowns a day because there's so much in her environment and daily routine that distresses her. I have parents who ask me, "Can you help me teach her that this is not a big deal?" And I say "No, but I can help you honor the fact that she thinks this is a big deal. Because if we tell her this is not a big deal and everything in her is saying it is a big deal, either her perceptions are wrong or you just don't get her. And when you don't resist her or make her wrong you teach her to trust herself and you teach her to trust you."

This is a sensitive person! Her reactivity may be an indicator that something's wrong – maybe she's not getting enough down time; maybe there are significant stressors in her home- or school environment; maybe she's not getting enough outside time. If she grows up experiencing her perspective as valid, she'll seek what she needs instead of getting sick because she denies the fact that she has needs. She'll also honor her intuition – she'll be able to say No to the guy who may be attractive, but something doesn't feel right.

Again, I'm not saying that changing your perspective is all you need to do. You do want the kid who's easily frustrated to learn that frustration is something that can be tolerated and managed. You want to show the sensitive kid how to troubleshoot a problem in his environment. You want to show the impulsive or bored kid how to manage that strong desire to move around, and you want to teach the strong-willed kid how to get what he wants in ways that respect others – because if these difficult personality traits are *undeveloped* strengths, certainly you need to develop them if your child is to benefit from them.

But when you see that stubbornness as a gift you're not trying to fix him or change him – *you simply want to develop that gift*. Because that stubbornness is a strength, you're not frustrated by it; instead, you honor it. Instead of telling him that he never listens, he's disrespectful, you would never have tried this kind of bad behavior with your dad, you say, Yeah, I get it – you really don't want to do that. Right now, you need to do it, because I've told you to do it. But let's talk about this tonight at a family meeting. Maybe we'll be able to come up with some ideas about how we can both get what we want. And when your kid hears that, he thinks, OK, my perspective is valid, but I also need to cooperate with my dad (and I also need to figure out how to convince him to see it my way).

When you can teach your child alternative, more productive behavior while also genuinely appreciating his bad behavior as the strength it represents, your child gets to experience the changes you want him to make as a movement toward greater capacity instead of a movement away from some deficiency. And when he sees that you respect his strength, he's actually going to want to work with you – he'll see himself as someone with something valuable to offer and he'll discover the pleasure that comes to someone who can share his strength in ways that work for everyone.

WOULD YOU LIKE A FREE TEMPERAMENT ASSESSMENT?

What is your child's temperament profile? A solid understanding of your child's temperament helps you to understand who she is and what she needs – and this will help you to relate to her in ways that mean less stress for the whole family. Would you like a free temperament assessment for your child? Go here (http://witsendparenting.com/tempassess) to set that up!

TANTRUMS

I want to talk about tantrums in this section because often one of the things that make parents think there's something wrong with their kid is the level of tantrum that a spirited kid is capable of. Parents will tell me, "Well, it's not what you're thinking when you think of tantrums. She can yell for 45 minutes and not stop." Or, "I don't know how long she can yell, the record is two hours but then I just gave in so she'd stop screaming."

But these are the kind of tantrums spirited kids can have. I can tell you, after having worked with hundreds and hundreds of kids as a teacher and/or counselor, that you're right – these tantrums are not typical of kids in general, but on the spirited end of the spectrum, they are common. Yes, it looks like they're going to bust a blood vessel or maybe have a stroke. But this is what expression and release looks like in kids with this level of energy and emotion. When something really hard happens in my life I might go to my room and cry, and my partner knows, Oh, she's expressing her feelings; it's OK. And expressing and processing is exactly what these kids are doing – they're just doing it on an atomic scale.

So when someone asks me, "How can I stop the tantrums?" I say, tell me about them, tell me what triggers them, because my goal is not to stop the tantrums; my goal is to help the child deal with these intense emotions, *in large part by simply normalizing them.* So the first thing we do is let the child know that tantrums are OK. We let them know that they are experiencing an emotion. The incredible, intense emotion is OK. Of course we need the kids to be safe. But the first step in dealing with tantrums is to relate to them as they are. There's nothing wrong with intense anger or frustration.

Anyway, you've already learned through hard experience that trying to stop the tantrums doesn't actually work. If you urge them to calm down, if you try to engage them in problem-solving, if you talk to them in a super-calm voice... OK, there are a lot of good books about mindfulness... maybe if you get her to take breaths and notice her body. But these things don't work with these kids because they are SO angry and SO frustrated, they're *compelled* to express it, and their brains are not in problem-solving mode. I've had parents tell me, "When he gets in that space I can't talk to him... It's like he's not even there." Well, think of it this way – he's there, but you're not there, you're *here*. And he's not rational, so if you want to connect with him, you need to start where he is.

Let's compare the tantrum to a huge fire. When your kid is having a meltdown, imagine that he's on the tenth floor of a burning building. Now if a firefighter wanted to get him out of that building she wouldn't stand at the bottom of the stairs and say Come on down. I'm the firefighter. I'm going to help, don't worry, we're putting the fire out – I just need you to come on down. No, the firefighter would go up to the tenth floor and *bring* your kid down. There are techniques you can use to show your child that you're there with him on the tenth floor, and things you can do to bring him down to the ground floor. But the first thing to do is accept the meltdown as normal and don't try to stop it. When you tell them to calm down or try to reason with them the message you give is that they are overreacting and you just don't get it.

Of course, "getting it" doesn't mean *you* have to suffer. Screaming and stomping are very different from hitting or kicking, or breaking furniture or hurting the cat. And there are things you can do to ensure that your child's meltdown is nonviolent, but the meltdown itself is valid and *may even be the most appropriate release the child has*, depending on where he is in his cognitive development.

A tantrum success story

Finally, I see so clearly that meltdowns are a valid and even necessary form of expression that I sometimes tell parents to trigger them. (This helps you to get them to happen at your chosen time and place :)) A while ago I had a 10-year-old whose parents were frustrated because their family routine included doing something fun on Saturdays – but every Saturday morning, right around the time everyone was ready to leave the house, this girl would pitch a fit and ruin the day. And I asked the girl, Really? Every Saturday morning? And she said, Yeah, I ruin it every Saturday morning. So it sounds like you need to have a fit every Saturday morning, I said. And the girl said, Yeah, I do.

Now, everybody in the family figured these outbursts were due to some mild mental health issue. But I said, OK, let's help you with this. What sets you off? "Well, I hate it when my mom comes in and tells me to clean my room because I'm tired and I don't want to do it." So we set it up so that Mom continued to tell her to clean her room every Saturday, but she made sure to tell her early, at 9:00 or 9:30. The girl then pitched a fit, and 45 minutes later everyone was in the car, off to have a wonderful day. So this family was able to get what they wanted by letting go of the question, How can we stop her meltdowns? In fact, this girl maintained an incredible schedule during the week. She loved everything she was doing, didn't want to give anything up, but she was also putting a lot of pressure on herself to do well in each of her activities. She was under a lot of stress – so, why not? Why not have a vent session every Saturday morning?

ANOTHER IMPORTANT PERSPECTIVE: WHAT CAN YOU SAY YES TO? BECAUSE OFTEN IT ISN'T SO BAD...

In the section above I shared a perspective that I believe is key to creating a supportive, collaborative, cooperative partnership with your spirited child – that is, those challenging personality traits and behaviors we see in spirited kids are strengths, not liabilities. In this section I'll share another important perspective. And this time we're going to see the good, not just in difficult traits like stubbornness or a hair-trigger temper, but also in behaviors almost *anyone* would define as "bad."

Before we get started, though, I do want to acknowledge that not all parents see bad behavior as bad behavior. Sure, they may find the behavior to be difficult, but their main response is one of compassion: "She must be really struggling or she wouldn't be acting this way. What do I need to do for her so she'll be in a more balanced place?"

On the other hand, there are also a lot of parents who are offended by their kids' behavior – and they find that behavior to be very, very frustrating. And for some parents, that frustration and anger is the main thing that brings them to me. If you're someone who is often angry with your kids, if you often find yourself yelling, scolding, criticizing, reprimanding – first, know that I *totally* get anger and I hold absolutely no judgment toward you. And I believe your frustration will decrease when you slow down and start to look for the good in your kid's bad behavior.

What I really mean by "looking for the good" is that it's very helpful to slow down, back up, and get clear about your child's perspective and intentions. Because often the intention is good, even when the behavior is unacceptable to us. As a kid I got into a *lot* of trouble for things that I thought were OK or even helpful, but they weren't. As an example, one time when I was doing the dishes I mistook the etching on my mom's new frosted mug for dirt. I tried to get the "dirt" off... first with a cloth... then with a scrubby... then with steel wool. I couldn't get it all off, though, so then I had to explain my "failure" to my mom. I was so afraid of her anger – and she was *very* angry – not because I couldn't clean the darned mug, but because I had marred the mug's appearance. "But I was trying to be good, Mom!"

Here's another example: One time when I was working with a family in their home their child got in trouble for "dumping" milk on the table. When we looked further, though, we learned that the boy was done with his bowl of cereal and, because it was a very bad thing to waste food in this family, he had tried to pour his unfinished milk back into the milk carton. He wasn't successful – he spilled the milk – but he hadn't just *dumped* the milk because that was a fun thing to do, or because he knew it would get a rise out of Mom. His intentions were good – he was trying to not waste food.

As I said above, some parents are always willing to give their kid the benefit of the doubt, but still, I've seen that it's awfully easy for adults to view innocent but unwanted behaviors as carelessness, thoughtlessness, selfishness, or defiance. It's also easy to over-fixate on the unwanted behavior when we're stressed – sleep-deprived, over-scheduled, we work too much, we don't have enough money... We don't need one more problem to solve or one more mess to clean up! But if we back up and see where the child is coming from, we may find that she wasn't being careless or oppositional. This will activate our empathy and reduce our frustration, and then we can use the problem as an opportunity to educate her, which both strengthens her and reduces the chance that the problem will happen again.

What about *really* bad behavior?

What about those times when it's pretty clear that the kid's intentions aren't so innocent? Let's use aggression as an example.

One time I was asked to work with a child who was interacting with her classmates in a less-than-appropriate way. She would bump into other kids, for example. Or she would walk through a play area in a way that disrupted the game the other kids were playing. She didn't act sorry when she did these things, so it was easy to view her behavior as inconsiderate or disrespectful. From the teacher's perspective, she was borderline-aggressive, disruptive, and annoying – but after I had spent some time observing the child, I saw that she was just really lacking in body awareness and awareness of the space around her. Now, I can appreciate that a teacher with 20 other kids might feel she has so much to manage that the main thing is just to stop the one disruptive kid. And we *did* stop the disruption – not by addressing so-called aggression or disrespect, but by learning what was actually causing the problem and then teaching her what she needed to know in order to overcome the problem.

Here's another example: One time I was asked to work with an older girl who kept getting into trouble for "always pushing" a classmate. From the teacher's perspective, the girl was aggressive and noncompliant. From my perspective, the girl was actually much more patient than I would have been in her circumstances! Because when I observed her I saw that as she was trying to do her work (the kids were supposed to be copying what the teacher was writing on the board), her classmate was taunting her: "You can't write." "You always have to look at my work." "You can't even copy right." And with each comment, the classmate (let's call her Kaylee) would move her chair more and more into my girl's space. Kaylee kept it up as my girl ignored her and continued to copy, until finally Kaylee had managed to move my girl right to the edge of the table. And then Kaylee inched even closer, and it was at this point that my girl responded. How? By pushing.

What we did in this case was put a piece of tape on the table; tell Kaylee that she was not to move her chair past the tape; and we also told my girl to raise her hand and ask for help when Kaylee crossed the line.

YOUR RULES ARE DUMB | 55

OK, I know that not all pushing and shoving occurs simply because some other child "started it," nor are all "aggression" issues solved this easily. But this is another example where a child's bad behavior was actually misinterpreted. My client wasn't trying to hurt or bully her classmate. Her continuing to push despite repeated correction by her teacher was not an act of defiance. Her parents had actually been baffled by the school reports because this girl is very patient. But there's only so much a person can take.

What if the first time the girl pushed her classmate the teacher had seen the behavior from her perspective? Probably she would have been less likely to label her as aggressive. What if the teacher had been less likely to label her as aggressive? Regardless of the type of label (whether negative or positive), *the way we see each other determines how we interact with them.* When you look beyond the difficult behavior to see what your child intended, you'll develop a broader, more positive perspective that will help you to address behavior problems in a way that lets her know you're on her side – and this will make her more willing to work with you.

WHAT ABOUT WHEN THE KID IS *TRYING* TO BE BAD?

I want to share one more example here because I want to show you how this practice of really looking at what's going on for the kid can help with even the most challenging behaviors.

Once I had a kid in my class who really *was* aggressive.

His aggression arose mainly in the context of conflict. So when there was disagreement, his go-to was violence. He especially liked to hit other kids with toys or other objects, and he hit hard enough to cause serious harm.

And this guy was also defiant. I tell the story that during his first few days with me he gave me no trouble whatsoever, because he was too busy just watching and observing how the class worked and what the rules were. And then, once he had it all figured it out, he went about breaking every rule in the book in a systematic, methodical way.

Without going into detail here, of course I *did* respond to his defiance with boundary-setting. I held him 100% accountable to follow class rules, physically helping him to do that when necessary. And I would intervene when I saw that he was about to strike another kid. But I was also able to work with him in other, really productive ways once I got clearer about what was motivating his behavior.

Now, teaching kids, developing and empowering them, is what I do, so it's natural for me to make the effort to understand the things that motivate them. But make no mistake. I did not assume this boy was like the two girls I described earlier in this section. It wasn't, "Oh, I'm sure his intentions are good," nor did I justify his behavior: "Oh, he must have suffered trauma at some point, that's why he's so angry." Still, once I had observed him for a while, I was able to view his behavior in a positive light. Specifically, I saw that his intentional defiance was his way of making an impact on the class, so making an impact was very important to him. He wanted to be seen as a force to be reckoned with. On the one hand you could interpret his behavior as, He wants it all his way and he wants to prove to the teacher that he'll have it his way. On the other hand, he's a kid – maybe he's simply saying, "Hey, I matter. I want control. I *do* have a lot of power – see?"

So I engaged him in using his power in constructive ways. I taught him to build things and together we decided he would build a boat for the class to play in. He built other things for the class as well, and after a while I had him teach the other kids how to use a saw, hammer, and drill. The other kids appreciated his contributions to their play and admired his work. And the ones who received his help with building listened to him and looked up to him. This boy *totally* loved all this positive attention, so for him, the building and teaching gave him an alternative, positive way to make an impact and be recognized. In turn, this alternative made it much easier for him to let go of his disruptive behavior.

IT HELPS WHEN YOU SEE WHAT'S REALLY HAPPENING

When you look beyond the bad behavior to see that behavior from your child's perspective, chances are this perspective will help you to respond with empathy (or even appreciation), so the behavior becomes much less frustrating. And when you see the impulse behind the bad behavior, whether that impulse is actually to be helpful or instead it's to be disruptive, you *really* enhance your ability to teach, guide, redirect, and ultimately empower your child. Because you're looking at more than just saying No to the problem, you're more able to focus on the learning opportunity the problem represents. And because you understand what causes the problem, you're able to solve the problem effectively. Do you think the aggressive, defiant boy in the last example would have responded to mindfulness or calming techniques? These would not have worked with him, because this guy wasn't all that stressed – he just wanted to make an impact.

And again, taking the time to see the problem from your child's perspective also shows your child that you're on his side, and this in itself increases his willingness to cooperate with you. One reason – not the *only* reason – but one reason kids resist is simply because it's natural to resist anyone who's speaking to us with anger and irritation. And kids' resistance and resentment become habitual when it feels like their parents correct them, not so much to really empower them, but more just to put an end to the parents' discomfort. And certainly kids feel resentful when they feel their intentions are misunderstood!

WHAT CAN *YOU* SAY *YES* TO?

If you're stymied by something your kid is doing and you're having trouble redirecting her, I can help you to find out where she's coming from. Let's start with a temperament assessment. It's free, and you can go here (http://witsendparenting.com/tempassess) to find out more about it!

BUT DON'T FORGET: YOU HAVE TO HAVE IT BOTH WAYS

On the other hand, as you reframe your kid's difficult personality traits as strengths and as you slow down to take a closer look at his problem behaviors, understand that "understanding" isn't enough! Understanding and connection loom large in much of the parenting advice out there nowadays, but for best results, yes, you *do* need to recognize your child's personality for the gift it is; you *do* need to understand what motivates his behavior – *and* you need to hold him accountable to do the right thing.

It's interesting for me to see this in action with so many different kids, how if you only focus on the empathy and connection, this connection feels totally right to them but it doesn't motivate them to change. Perhaps from the adult's perspective, it's a give-and-take: "I want your respect and consideration, so I'm going to give that to you." "I don't want to relate to you as a dictator, so I'll partner with you instead, and in turn you'll want to cooperate with me." We expect this kind of reciprocity from adults. But kids are in a *very* different place in their development. Kids are not looking at this from your perspective!

In my experience, kids are sponges for empathy, respect, validation, understanding... It feels good, and it makes perfect sense – "Hey, now you're starting to get me. Great! *I've* been getting me all along – and now *you're* starting to see me, too!" We're seeing them. And they're perfectly content with a relationship in which we keep seeing them, and seeing them, and seeing them... I worked with one very aggressive kid who had been through years of therapy, and every time he and I were in the middle of one of his violent outbursts he would comment – not because he was being defensive with me, but simply to explain – that he was angry and violent because he had experienced bullying in the past, etc. And then there was a defensive, older girl who hadn't had much understanding and acceptance in her family. I related to her in a compassionate and nonjudgmental way, and I acknowledged that her defensiveness stemmed from all the disapproval she had experienced in her family relationships. And after a while, whenever I would have a problem with her behavior and hold her accountable to do something different, it was "You know I don't respond to that!"

My point is that, from the boy's perspective, the appropriate response to a violent outburst was understanding, period. And the girl had developed an expectation that my interactions with her would always feel pleasant, and validating, and nurturing. My point is that for these kids – and most of the other kids I've known – understanding alone does not translate to an appreciation of the adult's need for certain limits, nor does it translate to an ability to tolerate and honor limits. Kids need both understanding and accountability if they are going to learn the values and behaviors you want to teach them.

5

PARTNERING WITH YOUR SPIRITED CHILD, PART II: TECHNIQUES

"I like talking this way. It works."

—Ten-year-old participant in one of the author's coaching programs

I've tried to distinguish between *technique* and *perspective* in this book, emphasizing the importance of perspective, because, although some tools and techniques are key, our perspective and mindset also play a huge role in the way we interpret and respond to our children's behavior. I described two perspectives that are key to developing a collaborative, cooperative relationship with your child in Chapter 4, and we'll be talking about specific parenting tools in the present chapter.

And we'll pay special attention to one tool in particular. Because there are a *lot* of different parenting tips out there – but if you Google it, you'll find that many so-called "positive discipline" tools are really part of a broader pattern of positive communication and connection with your child. Hugging, for example, or *encouraging, listening, respecting, complimenting, being kind...* And my purpose in these next sections is not to provide a catalogue of tips for relating to your child in a way that fosters connection, but rather to highlight one tool that a) gives your spirited kid an awesome venue for exercising autonomy and control and b) helps you to direct his strong will such that he's able to seek what he wants in constructive ways.

On the other hand, although we won't be focusing on connection per se, we will begin with it, because connection plays such a key role in motivating your child to really work with you and cooperate with you.

POSITIVE DISCIPLINE 101: CONNECTION

As one resource on Positive Discipline puts it, "Most of the Positive Discipline parenting tools provide skills for creating a connection" (see positivediscipline.com). Many parents today are quite familiar with the idea that it's best to address our kids' problem behavior with "positive," non-punitive, non-shaming responses, and Positive Discipline enthusiasts (and other connection-focused theorists) tell us that we cannot influence our kids in a positive way until we first connect with them.

It makes a lot of sense: Lecturing, nagging, blaming... scolding, belittling, shaming... all these create defensiveness. It's only natural to resist someone who's making you wrong. (Heck, it's natural to resist someone who's not making you wrong but they're still expressing frustration over something you did!) But when you relate to someone in ways that foster connection, that person is more likely to like you, trust you – and cooperate with you.

And here's something else about connection: As you know, connection is vital to human development. We have to have connection to thrive physically – for example, kids' connection with their parents boosts immunity and prevents disease, among other things. Connection is such a high priority for humans that a young human will do *anything* to get it – *and if a main way of connecting with parents and teachers is through conflict, kids will connect through conflict.* Some parents have asked me, "Why does she always push me to the edge? Wouldn't she rather not have me screaming at her?" Well, she could be pushing because she just needs contact, she just needs to have an interaction. I remember one time when I was eating out – I was watching this mother and her son at another table, and the mom was looking at her phone. And while she was interacting with her phone, her boy was poking her, trying to get her attention. Finally the mom asked, frustrated: "Why do you keep touching me?" And the boy answered, "I want you to stop touching your phone!"

Kids really want and need to connect with us, and even when parents are intentional about relating to their kids in ways that are never harsh or punitive, it can be hard to find the time to just connect. So make the time. I hope your family eats at least one meal together! (I think humans are probably hard-wired to bond when they're eating :)) It's also really effective when you connect right when you get home from work, or first thing in the morning, or last thing at night. And if you're someone who has very little down time, just take five minutes. Set aside five minutes to just be with your child. Tell stories about your day; take a little walk; or just sit quietly together. Just spending quality time together on a regular basis

– even if these times aren't long periods – will make a big difference in the quality of your relationship. And this will also ease any feelings of guilt or regret you may experience when your child responds to your boundary-setting with frustration and anger.

CONNECTION MISPERCEPTIONS

If you're reading this book, chances are you're a firm believer in the rightness of connection and the "wrong-ness" of interactions that are harsh or unkind. A lot of the parenting advice out there today centers on the power of connection, and along the same lines, a lot of experts tell us that a punitive approach makes parenting more difficult.

And I think these things are true. *But what is not true, in my opinion, is that all or most behavior problems are caused by a lack of connection.* And it is not true that connection is the only or main solution to bad behavior.

Yes, connection is key, but there are other factors besides connection at play; and as I stated earlier, some of the main factors in spirited kids' behavior are their energy, their emotional intensity, their strong will, and their desire for autonomy. All kids, but especially spirited kids, have a will of their own, and if your plans are not their plans, it is natural for them to push to have it their way.

Connection is one ingredient that impacts the degree to which your kid will resist you. So is your willingness to hold him accountable to listen to you. So is your ability to give him alternative venues for expressing his will. Because I work with a lot of families with spirited kids,

I talk to a lot of parents who are really distressed because they've done so much to connect with their child, but the behavior still continues, and to these parents this means they're not loving their child enough. In fact, they *do* love their child enough, but there's more to behavior than love and connection.

ANOTHER KEY TOOL FOR TRANSFORMING CHALLENGING BEHAVIOR: THE FAILPROOF FAMILY MEETING

In the sections above I agree that a positive connection with your child is a key factor in your child's behavior, but I disagree that connection is all there is to it. I'll be talking about another really important tool for transforming spirited kids' challenging behavior in the following sections. This tool is my Failproof Family Meeting – a structured family-meeting process that's especially effective with spirited kids.

Family meetings have several main benefits. Not only do they promote connection and bonding; they also teach kids (and parents) skills in positive, respectful communication; they provide a venue for peaceful problem-solving... *And one of the main benefits of the Failproof Family Meeting is that it gives parents a way to satisfy spirited kids' need for power and control. (And it's also specifically designed to address some of the challenges spirited kids bring to a family-meeting process.)*

WHY IT WORKS

More specifically, the Failproof Family Meeting is a tool for *sharing* power and control. When you have family rules and you hold your child accountable to listen to you but you also satisfy her need to exert her will, you remain in charge of the household, but you share your control with your child. And this sharing can be a big part of what makes your parenting "positive." It's what makes you a leader and not a despotic dictator. As a leader you still hold your kids accountable to follow you, but it isn't only "Do it because I said so." Instead, you're also asking your kids what *they* want. You're inviting them to help define the family's processes and protocols such that these important decisions are consistent with the kids' needs and preferences. Essentially, the Failproof Family Meeting enables kids to share in setting things up and/or share in solving problems in ways that work for everyone in the family. And in my experience spirited kids really appreciate and respect this sharing arrangement. Spirited kids are really awesome at collaborating, cooperating, and sharing power once they're taught to do this.

FAMILY MEETINGS 101

"Are you *sure* these work? 'Cuz we've tried family meetings..."

Family meetings – if they're done right – are *powerful*. And you can find a lot of good family-meeting templates and instructions in books and on the Internet – but it takes knowledge, skill and practice to become a truly effective facilitator. Really, running an effective family meeting – especially with spirited kids – is like "running" an effective psychotherapy session. There's more to it than the structure, and most skilled facilitators don't develop this skill just from a book or an outline. So as you read through and experiment with what I'll share here, don't worry if you experience gaps in your understanding. I'll point you to more information I have on my website, and I'll also share some videos that will answer some of your questions.

Some general points

--Do it weekly. Hold your family meetings weekly, even if you don't think you have anything to talk about. *This shows your kids that open communication and collaborative problem-solving are a priority.* It also provides a consistent space where, at least once a week, your family is going to slow down, sit down, and talk with each other. It lets the kids know that there's at least one time each week where you're going to be really listening to them and inviting them to tell you about something they want or something they'd like to change. Because the way we talk in family meetings is not the way we talk all the time. We're not always going to be in facilitator mode, in active listening mode... *and that's OK.* This is something I really like to emphasize with parents, that you shouldn't expect always to relate to your kids the way you want to in the family meeting. Over time the communication you'll be practicing will extend to many or most other areas in your life, but for now, just set aside that weekly space and stick with it.

--Sit at a table. Sitting at the kitchen table is best, or if you want to sit outside, sit in straight-backed chairs. I don't advise sitting on the couch because that encourages people to lay back and relax. The family meeting is a time when everyone should be sitting up, focusing, and paying attention.

--Keep meetings short – and grownups, keep comments brief. You can find more detailed "rules for grownups" on my website (http://witsendparenting. com/ffm), but I want to emphasize brevity here because meetings that run on too long and adults who talk too much can easily be experienced as boring and annoying – but we really want kids to like our family meetings. Remember, family meetings are *not* just a positive way to address specific behavior issues – one main reason we use family meetings with spirited kids is so we can show them more generally that this is a great space for using their voice and sharing power with parents. And this is why we want kids to really value these times – because it is these meetings that lay the foundation for the collaborative partnership you're creating. So keep your comments brief and let your kids do most of the talking: The more your kids actively participate, the more productive the meetings will be. Kids as young as two can benefit from family meetings – so how long should the meeting be if you have a 2-year-old as opposed to, say, a 14-year-old? See my website for details :)

--Respond to *all* ideas in a neutral and objective tone. As you're well aware, there are a number of positive-communication rules we follow in a family meeting. Active listening... responding in a respectful way... avoiding neg-atives like sarcasm or eye-rolling... but I want to highlight neutrality and objectivity in particular because a neutral, objective, calm response is another tool that shows kids that you are really listening to them, really taking them seriously – and thus truly willing to work with them in a collaborative way. *In fact, the neutral and objective tone is one of the most important aspects of the Failproof Family Meeting.*

As an example, let's say the family is trying to address the fact that Sara is always late for school because she won't get out of bed on time. And when it comes time to offer suggestions about how to solve this problem, Sara says that she should just stay home from school. When you don't *resist* or *dismiss* this suggestion as unacceptable or *gently explain* why it's unrealistic – and instead you respond objectively, writing it down and treating it just like any of the other suggestions being offered – you're telling Sara that you take what she says as real, intentional, and valid communication. And because her proposal is legitimate and something she's serious about, you are going to work with her. Now, this doesn't mean you're going to accept her proposal (and she may not actually be serious about the proposal, either – more on that later). But when you respond to her idea as well-intentioned and legitimate you tell her that you're really hearing her, you truly intend to honor her voice. And this satisfies (in part) her need for autonomy and choice.

--Let everyone facilitate. I describe the facilitator role in more detail on my website (http://witsendparenting. com/ffm), but for purposes of this chapter, once they get to the point where they can take this role on, have everyone in the family take turns as Meeting Facilitator. Having your child facilitate is a great way both to develop his listening skills and put him in a position of power. Children as young as four can facilitate if they've seen it done enough times! The only challenge with very young people facilitating is that the facilitator needs to be taking notes in order to track what everyone says. An older family member can handle this task if the facilitator is too young to do it.

--Use a "talking stone"; have everyone take turns; but don't force them to talk. Pick some object (a stone, a stick) to serve as a "talking stone," to help ensure that everyone can speak without being interrupted. And it's also important that the talking stone passes to each person in the group in a predictable, set order. So, for example, if the facilitator passes the stone to the person on her right, when that person is done talking she passes the stone to the person on her right, and so on. So if John passes the stone to Jamie on his right and then wants to respond to something Jamie said, *he has to wait until everyone else has had a chance to speak before he can make that response*. This shows the kids that *everybody* has the opportunity to be heard, every time. It can encourage the quieter members of the group to speak up, and it prevents the "talkers" from simply passing the stone back and forth among themselves.

What if the person who has the stone says they have nothing to say? Don't force it – let them pass. You'll see what I mean as you read further below.

--Make the first meeting super-easy. At your first family meeting, don't say to your kids, "Hey, everybody, we're going to have a Family Meeting. Now, come and sit down. Let me tell you how this is going to go..." Because your kids don't yet know how valuable these meetings are going to be. And at first they're likely to resist the idea of "The Family Meeting."

So make the first few meetings easy and attractive: "Hey everybody, let's sit down and decide what we want to have for dessert." Or, "Let's decide what movie we're going to see." Any topic that's not controversial, where it won't be too hard to come to agreement. As you get a little practice you'll be able to have more serious conversations, but establish the basic patterns with two or three meetings that focus on fun topics.

THE FAILPROOF FAMILY MEETING,
STEP-BY-STEP

Now I'm going to give you an overview of each step in the Failproof Family Meeting process. This will show you how the process should go – but know, too, that meetings can vary significantly depending on your child's age – and temperament.

You'll find that really young kids need to be exposed to family meetings for a time before they're able to follow each step in the way we might want them to. And it may also take a few weeks before your child chooses to participate in meetings in a genuine, productive way. Often this is because it just takes time for him to understand that his voice truly is an important part of the family's decision-making processes. And this happens even when parents go out of their way to show their kids that they take their perspective and feelings into account. So it's not that you haven't listened to your child or taken him seriously, but often parents don't take the time to really involve their kids in problem-solving and decision-making in a structured way and on a regular basis, and kids need time to get used to this process.

So if at first it doesn't look like family meetings are working, don't give up! Remember, the Failproof Family Meeting is about much more than any one or five or fifteen meetings – these meetings are actually a *long-term, weekly practice* that helps your family to connect, work together, and solve problems in a collaborative way. And like a lot of practices, this one requires skills that are developed over time. If you feel like your meetings aren't working the way you want them to, my website (http://witsendparenting.com/ffmvideos) has several videos that answer some frequently-asked questions. Finally, as I describe the Failproof Family Meeting I'll also tell you about something *most other experts don't talk about*: How to continue the meeting when your kids aren't participating – or when they're actively refusing to come to agreement.

Step 1: Open the meeting and share some good news

The first step in the Failproof Family Meeting is simply to offset the meeting with some kind of Meeting opening and then start things off on a happy note. Open the meeting by singing a song, or maybe you'll want to light a candle. Or, maybe you'll just say, "Now we're going to have our Family Meeting."

Open the meeting, thank everyone for coming, and then ask everyone to take a turn sharing, for example, something that made them laugh that week. Or something they like about their family. Or everyone can share their favorite joke. It's nice if your question prompts participants to share about something another family member did – for example, "What's something someone else did this week that you're proud of?" – because this gives people practice in looking for the good in others. But the main thing is just to get people focused on something positive – kind of like an ice-breaker.

Step 2: Agree on a topic

The topic to be discussed in the family meeting is chosen in Step 2. And note that in this step, *topic* does not mean *problem* – problems are described in Step 5. So, for example, if I'm having a problem with Joey not getting to bed on time, I'm not going to say "I need Joey to get to bed on time." Instead, I'm going describe my topic as "Bedtime." As another example, if I'm concerned because my child is not eating enough vegetables, I'm not going to state that concern in Step 2. Instead, I'll suggest that we talk about eating a wider range of foods. As another example, if I feel that my kids watch too much

TV, in Step 2 I'll introduce a topic like "Screen-time." If your child frames a topic as a problem you can reframe the problem as a topic and then ask him if your reframe is a good description of his topic.

If you have younger kids you'll probably be the one who's introducing most of the topics, but *always* ask: "What do you want to talk about?" Write each topic down, even if your daughter says "I want to get a pony" and you think a pony is absolutely out of the question. Remember, it's important to take every idea seriously, so treat every idea as valid – *and you may even want to have everyone practice this beforehand*. Warn your kids: "OK, now I'm going to ask you to do something really hard," and then mention a topic you know they won't love – and each person's job is to accept the idea without rolling their eyes, saying the topic is stupid, making sounds that convey disgust or contempt, etc.

Choose one topic per meeting – and for the first, say, eight meetings, focus on the kids' topics as often as you can. One exception to this one-topic rule would be if you have a very young child whose idea is not really a point of discussion; it's just a topic she's interested in (*Princesses*, for example). In this case, have everyone say something about the topic she raised so she can experience the family discussing something that's important to her. Then move on to the main topic.

How do you actually decide on a topic? The goal is to reach a consensus, so once you have your list of topics, ask everyone to share which topic seems most important. Sometimes people will agree that the topic that should be discussed is a topic someone else has raised. But if there is no consensus... well, this is where facilitation skills come in.

One strategy that's firmly in line with the broader goal of solving problems in a collaborative way is to have everyone respond to questions like "How should we decide which topic is most important?" Or (as a genuine question), "Why should your topic have the highest priority?" And you may be able to let your high-priority topic wait (to facilitate consensus) if you let the group know that you'll be the sole decision-maker in the interim: "Well, nutrition is really important to me. I'm willing to let it go and talk about the pony tonight but I want to let you know that I'm not going to be buying any more ice cream until we talk about nutrition." In the beginning choosing a topic will be easier if you and your co-parent have agreed on your topic ahead of time. And again, I also have parents suggest an attractive and easy topic for the first few meetings.

Now, you may be asking, Why is Step 2 Picking a *Topic*? Why not get right to the problem? You're right: Before getting to the problem I have families agree on a topic – and also move through Steps 3 and 4 – because this lowers kids' resistance. Lowering kids' resistance (in an inconspicuous way) is another key piece of the Failproof Family Meeting, and my structure includes multiple steps where everyone gets to spend a little time sharing and being heard in a context that is non-threatening. So yes, in Step 2, topics are neutral. They aren't controversial – they're just topics. This reduces defensiveness, and again, when you give spirited kids a space where they can just talk and be heard, you meet their need to have influence and choice.

Step 3: Discover what's important

Step 3 helps your family to gain an understanding of what everyone needs or prefers in relation to the chosen topic. Step 3 lets everyone know each other's broader, more general needs and values related to the topic, *and in turn this gives everyone information they can use to evaluate the proposals made during the meeting's problem-solving phase.*

Let's say the topic is bedtime. "What's important to you about bedtime," the facilitator asks. You might say that it's important to you that your child gets enough sleep. Or you might say that it's important that bedtime be early, so you and your co-parent can spend some time together without the kids. On the other hand, your child might say that bedtime should be late – because this gives her more free time to do whatever she wants to do.

As another example, in a discussion about chores or housework, you might say that you think it's important that everyone shares in the work. Or if the topic is getting to school on time, you might say that being late for school makes you late for work, and it's important that you get to work on time.

As you can probably imagine, preferences, general needs and values can start to sound like problems, depending on how you frame things. But the purpose of Step 3 is simply to provide a structure that allows everyone to see each other's needs and preferences in a more neutral light. Stating more general preferences before you get to the problem-solving stage gives you a particularly effective way to facilitate genuine collaboration: Step 3 moves the conversation away from "I want X." "Well, I want Y!" and sets things up so that, when your child proposes a solution like, "Bedtime should be 11:00," you can say, "OK, you think bedtime should be at 11. How does your proposal meet my need for you to get enough sleep?"

Step 3 can be a hard step for kids to understand, so you may need to probe a little: "Why do you want that?" "What do you like about that?" Accept their answers and just be open to whatever they tell you; they'll understand Step 3 in time.

Step 4: Repeat what the person next to you said in Step 3

Step 4 gives everyone a chance to develop their listening skills: In Step 4, each person repeats what the person on their left (or right – the facilitator decides) said in Step 3. And if Sally doesn't remember what the person on her left said, she should ask the person to say it again. And then that person should simply repeat themselves, without elaborating, so the focus moves right back to Sally. And if Sally "remembers" what her neighbor said but doesn't repeat what that person actually meant, that person should say, "That's not what I meant" and then clarify. And then Sally should repeat that person again.

If someone doesn't remember what their neighbor said, they probably weren't really listening, right? But *don't* say, "You're not listening, you never listen; this is why we tell you to listen; why can't you listen..." Just have them ask the other person to repeat themselves as many times as they need to. This part of the process is really important because it helps kids learn through experience that your words have meaning, they have real concepts attached to them. They're not just sounds ("Mwa mwa mwa...") to be tuned out, and they're not always directives to be obeyed. You have more to say to them than "Do this" or "Stop doing that!"

Step 4 also gives kids another opportunity to experience you taking them seriously. Because in the Failproof Family Meeting you're going to be responding to everything everyone else says in a neutral way, right? So if in Step 3 everyone was sharing what was important to them in a dessert and your 9-year-old said, "It's important to me that dessert be something I'm never allowed to have," in Step 4 you say, simply: "For you, dessert should be something you're never allowed to have." Of course, inside you're going to be experiencing a total disconnect. But it's important that you don't dismiss these kinds of statements. Simply repeat what your kid said as though it's entirely valid. Because repeating what he said does not mean you have to *do* what he said, and when you treat every idea as valid, you tell him that he really does have a place at the table, and you respect whatever he brings.

Step 5: State the problem

Step 5 is where your family gets clear about the problem(s) or decision point(s) associated with the topic you chose in Step 2. Again, when you want to solve a problem in a family meeting, *this* is where you state the problem – you don't state it in the Topic phase.

Now, you might be thinking that the person who had introduced the topic is now the one who gets to reframe the topic as a problem. And this is another advantage of Fail-proof Family Meetings: Because they were designed with spirited kids in mind, they place extra emphasis on teaching kids that everyone has a voice, everyone's ideas are valid, and everyone gets to negotiate for whatever it is they want. This being the case, every person at the meeting gets to state whatever problem they may have about the topic.

So if the topic is The Food Our Family Eats and Mom had introduced that topic, her problem could be that the kids aren't eating enough vegetables; Adrian, her picky eater, might say that meals include too many things he doesn't like; Dad might not have a problem with the topic, so he would pass the talking stone; and Sara might simply say something funny about food and she would pass the stone. If you think about it, it's entirely possible to design solutions (Steps 6 and 7) that take multiple problems into account, so if your family finds that it has several problems related to the topic, simply write these problems down, and move to the next step. Remember, you're going to be neutral and accepting of whatever people say they want!

Finally, just as in the topic-selection phase, the language you use is so important! So here are some examples of the way you want to state problems:

- Problem: "We're late for school almost every day" – *not* "You refuse to get up when it's time to get up" (Topic: "Getting ready for school/work in the morning")

- Problem: "You aren't getting enough vegetables in your diet" – *not* "You're too picky" (Topic: "Eating a wider range of foods")

- Problem: "I think the amount of TV I'm letting you watch is too much" – *not* "You watch too much TV" (Topic: "Screen-time")

Step 6: Brainstorm solutions to the problem

Step 6 does just what its name says it does: It provides a space for brainstorming. In Step 6, people make suggestions about how to solve the problem(s) described in Step 5, but they're encouraged to do this in a creative, spontaneous way. Step 6 is another step that's explicitly intended to lower resistance and give kids another opportunity to be heard without being evaluated. And because this step is all about free expression, it also helps kids get some of their silly or wildly unrealistic suggestions out of their system! So if the problem is We're Often Late for School and the (suggested) solution is Let's Attend Disneyland Instead of School, no worries! As always, just respond to all ideas in a calm and neutral way. And when everyone is through brainstorming, the facilitator (who's written everyone's ideas down) should *read* everyone's ideas in that same objective tone. Then, move on to Step 7.

Step 7: Make a proposal

Step 7 is the "official" decision-making stage. In this step everyone shares what they feel are their best suggestions for what to do about the issues raised up to this point. And because Step 7 is about decision-making as opposed to brainstorming, there will be some evaluation of the ideas presented in this step. More specifically, *the changes decided on in Step 7 should be ones that fit with what everyone said in Step 3 (What's Important?) and Step 5 (What's the Problem?).* As in the brainstorming stage, kids' proposals may continue to be unrealistic (to put it mildly) – but remember, discuss each proposal as if it were legitimate. How can you accept "unacceptable" proposals and still end up with an acceptable solution? Here is one example of what Step 7 might look like:

Let's say everyone has been talking about the food the family eats. Once Step 6 is complete, 16-year-old John, the facilitator, asks the person on his right if she has a proposal related to the topic: "Sara, do you have a proposal?"

Sara: I want to eat my coloring books.

Facilitator: OK, you want to eat your coloring books [facilitator writes Sara's statement down on the paper he's using to track everyone's contributions]. Adrian [Adrian is on Sara's right], do you have a proposal about the food the family eats?

Adrian: I think we should eat out, so everyone can order what they want. I don't like a lot of the foods we eat. [Adrian passes the stone to Mom, who's sitting to his right.]

Mom: I want us to eat more vegetables. I propose that I serve vegetables first, and we eat them before we eat the main dish. [Mom passes the stone to Dad, who's sitting to her right.]

Dad: I think Mom's idea is more practical than eating out every night. But instead of serving the vegetables first, I think we should say that people don't get dessert unless they've eaten all their vegetables. [Dad passes the stone to the facilitator, who's sitting to his right.]

Adrian: I don't want more vegetables!

Facilitator: Oops! Adrian, remember what we're supposed to do when someone says their idea? Let's try that again. Dad, could you say your idea again? [Dad repeats himself and Adrian doesn't respond. The facilitator jumps in, quickly.]

Facilitator: Good job, Adrian! I like Dad's idea, but I don't love vegetables either so I'd like to talk about which ones we're going to eat. [Facilitator passes the stone to Sara.]

Sara: I think we should have more corn. [Sara passes the stone.]

Adrian: I hate vegetables and I want to eat out at night.

Now, at this point you can see how the facilitator, Sara, Mom, and Dad might easily reach a consensus. For example, Mom could propose that they go with Dad's idea and also be sure they eat plenty of corn and whatever other vegetables people prefer. But Adrian's proposal doesn't fit. How do we handle that? We don't want to invalidate him, so one way to address this would be for Mom (she's on his right so she gets the talking stone) to work with the idea in a way that prompts him to explore other possibilities:

Mom: "Well, it would be nice to eat out every night, but that's really expensive, and I don't want to spend our money that way. And how does that meet my need to have you eat more vegetables?" *But remember, Adrian does not get to respond just yet.* Everyone gets an equal chance to speak, so the stone passes to Dad, the facilitator, and Sara before Adrian makes his response: "Well, I hate vegetables. And I also don't like spaghetti."

And here's where the facilitator might try to lead Adrian to make a suggestion that moves the group forward: "Adrian, you hate vegetables and spaghetti. What do you think of the proposal we have now to eat vegetables before dessert and to have corn once a week?"

Adrian: No.

Facilitator: Adrian, we want you to help us to come up with a solution that meets everybody's needs. Mom needs for us to eat more vegetables, I want us to choose which ones we're going to eat, and Sara wants more corn. We want to work with your ideas, but if you can't give us an idea that helps everyone get what they want, we'll have to make the decision without you.

Depending on your child's intentions and attitude your family's conversation might go any number of ways, *but this last response is one you can always give when a child is reluctant to participate with a genuine intention to meet everyone else half-way.* Or the child might not *want* to resist the process – but, like a lot of us, it's easier to get defensive and fight what he *doesn't* want, as opposed to imagining something he could live with, that also gives everyone else some of what they want. But in the Failproof Family Meeting – although it's a space that gives everyone the chance to participate in decision-making on an equal footing – *everyone's needs are taken into account.* Therefore, if someone's decision does not give everyone some of that they want, this is just not the way we do it in our family meeting, and the other participants can make another decision.

To keep the example above fairly simple, let's say that everyone was able to come to agreement. In the course of the meeting Mom reminded Adrian of three vegetable dishes he was OK with, and in the end everybody agreed to an arrangement that would get the family eating more vegetables. In this case we can move on to Step 8.

Step 8: Formalize the agreement

Once everyone has agreed on a decision, it's time to essentially formalize the agreement and bring the meeting to a close. So at this time the facilitator asks the group to confirm their agreement: "Does everybody agree that our vegetables are going to include a lot of corn, asparagus and snap peas, and we don't get dessert if we don't eat our vegetables?" If everyone still agrees to this, the facilitator writes the agreement on a piece of paper and asks everyone to sign it. And that document is posted on the refrigerator or a bulletin board. And then it's nice to conclude with a song, or maybe a board game – or you could just say, "Thank you for coming to the Family Meeting."

This kind of formal conclusion ensures that everyone understands the agreement and writing it down gives you something you can refer to later if need be. What if the topic was simple, or fun, and you know no one is going to forget or change their mind about the decision? You still want to go through Step 8 because you want that consistency and also, the decisions your family makes are going to get bigger and bigger. At some point you might be talking about a pony or a car for your kid and you want to be very clear about the conditions under which you're going to have that pony or new car.

But what if we can't get through Step 7?

Consensus sounds magical, but it's not easy and it's not always pretty. Not everybody gets everything they want in a consensus – they've just agreed to agree. And that's a pretty advanced concept for a 4-year-old or a 16-year-old.

So if you can't agree on a decision in Step 7, don't worry about it, and say something like, "OK, we did not get to a decision on this tonight. When should we revisit this? At our next meeting? Do you want to revisit this tomorrow?"

Remember, ultimately the Failproof Family Meeting is not as much about reaching specific agreements as it is a *practice* that gives your child a space for exerting his will in a constructive way. So reassure everyone: We *are* going to come to a conclusion. And invite everyone to think about the issue in the meantime – and also let everyone know that we aren't going to talk about the problem outside the Family Meeting. This gives the decision real importance and it also discourages arguments and bickering about the issue in the interim.

Now, I know that, especially with some topics, it might be real tempting to just take over: "OK, fine, I'll make the decision: Here's what we're gonna do..." But if you do that you run counter to everything family meetings are about. As the parent you're in charge and it's great that you're willing to *be* in charge, but family meetings are a special space where everyone shares power – so don't use *your* power to bypass the agreement process!

On the other hand, you don't have to let chaos reign, either. Again, it is perfectly OK to say something like, "Well, we've been talking for 45 minutes and we aren't going to get to a decision tonight. This is an important issue, and until we come to an agreement we're going to keep things the way they are [or just state a new rule if you can't live with the way things are]. But when do you want to revisit this? In our next Family Meeting?"

WHEN KIDS REFUSE TO PARTICIPATE

The family meeting process I've described above sounds fairly straightforward, but when you have really strong-willed or oppositional kids, it can get difficult pretty fast. This being the case, a lot of the parents I work with find that they benefit from some training in the Failproof Family Meeting. In this training I help parents develop their listening- and objectivity skills and I also show them how they can empower their kids and share decision-making with the kids *while preventing the kids from taking over the meeting.*

And although above I gave examples of ways to respond to some of the challenges kids pose, I'll also talk more about these challenges in this section. Because *most if not all of what I've read about family meetings does not address the resistance that strong-willed kids can bring to the process.* Family meetings are often listed as a Positive Discipline tool, and I completely agree with the premise of Positive Discipline – but spirited, strong-willed kids don't necessarily respond to active, reflective, respectful listening in the cooperative ways we'd like.

Some of the main challenges parents encounter include kids giving silly or unrealistic responses, or telling you they have nothing to say, or responding to questions with a sulky, "I don't know," or responding in a snarky, sarcastic tone. I also have a lot of parents tell me that their kid "just won't negotiate." These kids come to meetings saying, essentially, "It's my way or no way" – they veto any suggestion that's different from their own. Or, instead of outright refusing to accept others' proposals, the kid may argue with these proposals or present an unacceptable alternative using facts and logic parents find hard to answer. You see this one a lot with older kids.

So how do you deal with these challenges? *Read on, because the Failproof Family Meeting includes elements that are designed specifically to lead spirited and strong-willed kids to participate in a genuine way.*

For example, the rule that it's OK for anyone to pass gives parents an "out" when kids say that they have nothing to say. This rule means that parents don't need to struggle to get a response, and forcing a response wouldn't work anyway, right? So instead you can say, "Oh, you want to pass? OK." And if the child continues to not participate, you should let him know: "It's OK to pass, but if you don't contribute, we'll make the decision without you." So here we have parents' non-resistance coupled with a key Family Meeting rule: *If someone doesn't contribute to or participate in the meeting in a meaningful way, the others can make the decision without him.* The child doesn't *have* to participate, but his refusal to participate is not going to derail the meeting.

The two main factors that facilitate spirited kids' meaningful contribution to family meetings are a clear understanding that true participation ultimately comes down to real cooperation; and parents' neutral, non-resistant, non-judgmental tone. As I described above, I ask parents to use a neutral tone and always, always *always* refrain from judging or correcting others' statements – not simply to promote connection, but mainly to show kids that parents are taking them seriously. And this is a main reason we engage in Step 4. You have to be very intentional and diligent about this neutral, calm acceptance, and it usually takes some time, but *strong-willed kids respond very well once they really get it that their ideas will be received and respected.*

Again, though, although you listen, you're very respectful, you treat every idea as valid, if the child doesn't participate, decisions get made without him – *and partic-ipation is defined as genuine collaboration and cooperation.* And this is your end response to silly responses, unrealistic responses, or outright refusals to work with other people's ideas. Essentially, you hold a boundary: You'll share your decision-making power with your child, but it is not going to be his way or no way. And he doesn't get to derail the meeting. *You'll share the decision-making power, but you're still in charge.*

This blend of power-sharing and parental authority teaches kids to get their voice out there in an honest conversation that moves *everyone* forward, and kids learn that this feels good! They find that the price of giving a little is worth the respect and choice that come with it. It feels good to have an equal voice. It also feels good to work with each other in a way that takes everyone's needs into account, because when you do that, you're not just taking, you're also contributing. And spirited kids really *do* enjoy contributing, once they're taught to do it; and they have some really good ideas. I see this again and again in my practice.

More examples

Here are some more examples of some of the challenges kids can pose in family meetings, along with my suggestions for dealing with them:

--Silly, "non-responses." One time I was facilitating a meeting for a family with a picky eater. This girl – Jenny – was four. The topic was eating new foods, and of course the parents' problem was that Jenny always rejected new foods. During the meeting's proposal stage the family basically agreed that everyone would eat one new food that week, so I asked everyone to go around and name some new foods they might like to try. But what did Jenny want to try? *Towels.* So I said, "OK, towels." And I wrote that down. And the next time the talking stone came around, Jenny wanted to try *Hair*. So I said, OK, hair; and I wrote that down. And then I said that we would make a list and, per the agreement, everyone would try something from the list that week. And at this point Jenny saw that we really were going to just take her responses at face value, and she asked, "Wait – can we go around again?" So we went around again, and this time, she said, "Cheese." This is a classic example of a child in the process of learning that her contributions matter. It also shows how kids change their behavior to participate more honestly as they see that their responses will be honored (and along the same lines, they won't get what they want if they don't ask for it).

--**"My way or no way."** I gave an example of this challenge when I described Step 7. As another example, if in the meeting everyone is talking about what we eat for breakfast and a kid insists on a food that doesn't fit with the preferences people shared in Step 3, your first response would be to remind him that his proposal does not take into account something that someone else finds important. Then – assuming, for example, that it's important to someone that breakfast be nutritious – you can invite him to make a proposal that meets that person's needs, or if he doesn't want to do that, you'll make the decision without him. You can also choose to continue the conversation later, saying something like, "OK, ice cream is too far away from what's important to me – I need breakfasts to be nutritious. We can't get to a consensus with ice cream, so we won't make a decision at this meeting. In the meantime, though, I will decide what's for breakfast. Do you want to talk about this again at our next meeting?"

--**Challenging arguments.** One time I was facilitating a meeting with a 14-year-old boy and his parents. The parents wanted to reach an agreement about cell phone use, but the boy, who didn't want his phone use restricted, asked why he couldn't just make his own rules about the phone. "Because you're still a kid and besides, we're paying for it," his parents answered. And then the boy argued that he should make the rules because he planned to get a job and take over the payments.

These parents found this argument challenging because they placed a very high value on supporting their son's autonomy, and they also loved that he would be taking on more responsibility. And the boy's argument made some sense. Still, they didn't want zero limits on cell phone use!

In fact, though, the boy's response amounted to an introduction of a new, complex issue that's a wonderful topic for a Family Meeting: "If I pay for it, I control it." Clearly, this assumption is one that should be explored in detail – because, for example, what if he buys a car in a few years? Does this mean he gets to go wherever he wants, whenever he wants? Should we change the law to allow him to run red lights, because he paid for his car? In this case one effective response would be to name the argument for what it is – an issue to be addressed at another meeting. In the meantime – assuming everyone has already agreed on cell phone use as a topic – the agenda is to reach an agreement about cell phone use. Given the boy's unwillingness to accept restrictions, it may take several meetings before an agreement is reached. In the meantime, then, the parents can make the rules about the phone.

The Family Meeting: "Our way or my way" (*not* "My way or no way")

The Failproof Family Meeting is an incredible tool that, when used correctly, provides a number of key benefits. These meetings meet spirited kids' very real need for power and choice. They give kids a chance to contribute to the family policies and decisions that are important to them. They provide an opportunity for parents to teach kids negotiation and collaboration. They develop empathy and build listening-skills. Bottom line, they are an excellent tool for teaching and motivating spirited kids to cooperate.

On the other hand, if you're actually going to *see* these benefits, the family meeting needs to run its intended course, right? There must be equal space for everyone, there must be consensus about the topic, and there must be consensus about the end decisions that are made. But it's natural for kids to resist family meetings at first, and strong-willed kids are especially good at derailing them. For most kids, in fact, consensus is not a priority.

And this is why I tell parents that you can't have meaningful consensus with spirited kids if you haven't established yourself as the one in charge of the household. To put it another way, strong-willed or oppositional kids will sabotage the meeting every time if parents are not comfortable using their authority to say, It's not going to be *your way or no way* – it's going to be *our way or my way*: If we can't reach a solution that meets everyone's needs, I'll make the decision.

And this brings us back to one of the main themes of this book: Collaboration is the main goal, but you can't get there without accountability. This stance is different from that of those experts who would have us use the Family Meeting – collaboration and consensus – as a *substitute* for accountability. *But this substitution doesn't work with oppositional kids, because, essentially, if you don't hold oppositional kids accountable to collaborate, they are not motivated to do it.*

And this is why I don't teach parents how to run a Failproof Family Meeting until they have first gotten very good at holding their kids accountable to listen to them. Because if they don't listen to you when you tell them to hang up their coat, they won't listen to you when you hold the line: Shared decision-making depends on participation, and participation is defined as cooperation. When parents try family meetings before the kids learn to listen, the kids are much less likely to cooperate; parents are more likely to engage with them in frustration and anger; the meeting won't go as intended; and parents will conclude that family meetings don't work. They *do* work, and kids respond to them, but you have to be the leader who can take charge and see it through.

Don't worry, though. Kids really do value "our way."

The image below is a copy of a note one my young clients left for me :) And because the last few sections focused so much on kids' resistance to family meetings, I want to take a minute here and emphasize that kids' resistance really does decrease after they've had some experience with the process.

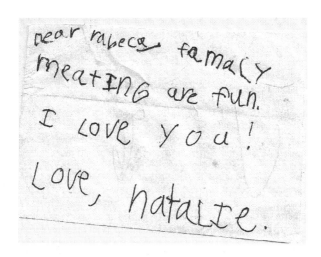

Note from a young client who loves the Failproof Family Meeting!

I've seen over and over in my work with strong-willed, spirited kids, that having a voice in important decisions is really meaningful for them. I remember how, at one of the meetings I facilitated, the boy was reluctant to come to the session at first – he was pretty young and didn't want to sit at a table. "You don't have to come," I told him – "but tonight we're going to be talking about bedtime, and I think your parents want to talk about the number of books they read to you. I don't know what they want to choose [a white lie], but if you want to have a say you might want to come." And then the boy looked over at his parents, paused for a second, and said, "I want to come to the Family Meeting." As another example, I'm currently working with a 10-year-old girl who's had a history of hitting and kicking her mom when she's frustrated, and her mom and I have also been working with her resistance to household chores. And after a recent family meeting in which we continued to focus on these problem behaviors, she said, "I like talking this way. It works."

As you well know, kids *could* choose to resist and resist and resist no matter what. They *could* respond to collaborative problem-solving with, "OK, make the decision without me. And when it comes time for you to implement, I'll just fight it, like I always do." But they like having a place at the table, and if they need to use their voice in positive, productive ways to have that place, they'll do it. And kids are social creatures. They may not come into the world knowing how to cooperate and collaborate, but once they're taught to do this it totally grows on them. I believe they get it intuitively that cooperation is a gift, a way of contributing to the family, and I think the vast majority of humans are hard-wired to feel good when they contribute. And in my experience, kids who learn to problem-solve in ways that work for everyone take on even more responsibility and contribute in even bigger ways.

AND I'M HERE TO HELP IF YOU NEED IT

Have you tried Family Meetings at your house yet? How's it going? As I mentioned earlier, a lot of the parents I work with find that they benefit from training in Family Meetings. You can access video that answers frequently-asked questions by going here (http://witsendparenting.com/ffmvideos) – and go here (http://witsendparenting.com/ffmcourse) to learn more about my Family Meeting course!

AND FINALLY: MAKE A GOOD THING BETTER...

As my emphasis on family meetings and collaborative problem-solving suggests, I believe that kids are much more willing to cooperate when they're invited to participate in decisions about what's expected of them. Participation is important. When we participate, we're a part of things, and we tend to want to contribute to that which we're a part of. And family meetings are one way for kids to participate alongside their parents. *And ultimately, kids will become even more willing to work with you if you have them participate in other ways, too.*

What I'm getting at here is participation in the work a family must do – participation in the effort that's needed to keep the household going. In most cases, this simply means *participation in household chores.*

I talk to a lot of parents who feel that it's somehow punitive to ask kids to do chores, but if you think about it, sharing in the household work makes sense. Does it really feel right when everyone gets to eat, but only one or two people cook and clean? Does it really feel right when the kid shares in the decisions that are important to the family, but he doesn't share in the family responsibilities? I'm not actually focused on fairness, here – but kids' participation in household chores *does* put them in a stronger position at the negotiating table. In my experience, parents just feel better about their kids when kids share in the work: It's easier to compromise with someone who's carrying part of the load.

"Well, I don't need my kids to carry the load," some parents say. "He's a kid. He has homework – *that's* his work. He doesn't need to worry about anything else." But – and this is the more important point – when kids contribute to the larger group, this develops their sense of their place in that group. It enhances their sense of belonging. It gives them a stronger sense of purpose. It shows them that they *really matter* – not in some abstract sense, simply because you love them, but because their family depends on them to get certain things done. They're contributing to the wider group in a concrete way, and this builds their self-esteem. And because this kind of contribution enhances their sense of importance and belonging, when kids share in the household chores, they become even more willing to cooperate with you and collaborate with you.

And this is why I'm talking about this in this part of the book. Because for me, doing household chores is not just a rule you should enforce because this teaches kids basic skills and teaches them responsibility and instills a work ethic, etc., etc. Chores do all this, to be sure, but for me the most important thing is that *chores themselves enhance kids' willingness to participate in the family in a positive, cooperative way.*

In the beginning, of course, you do have to hold kids accountable to do chores. Kids don't start out thinking that sharing in the work is a great idea because it will build their self-esteem. And along the same lines, I believe you *should* hold kids accountable to do chores – because you don't get the benefits I'm describing here when you simply *invite* kids to contribute. Kids need to feel that their contribution is necessary, that the family *must* be able to depend on them. They won't feel that way if it's, "Hey, I'd like it if you did this, would you like to do it? (It's OK if you say No...)" Kids are not going to develop a stronger sense of commitment to the family if chores are something they can do or not, it's up to them, because for one thing with this kind of arrangement they're not likely to do them. And this kind of Do-you-want-to? arrangement doesn't convey the sense that their participation is essential.

How do you get your kids to do chores? Should kids get paid to do chores? (No – they should do chores because they're a part of the family and everyone in the family contributes to the work that needs to be done.) How old should a kid be before we ask him to do chores? What kind of chores are best for younger kids? I'm not going to get into these details in this book, but you can go here (http://witsendparenting.com/choresbyage) for more information on age-appropriate chores. And a "chores certification program" is one really fun way to motivate spirited kids to do chores. You can go here (http://witsendparenting.com/chorescert) to learn more about that.

CONCLUSION

"A happy family life requires both parents and kids to be empowered at the same time."

–Rebecah Freeling

When I met 10-year-old Emma for the first time, she was sitting on the couch with her mother, scowling like a thundercloud. Her mother had reached out to me because she wanted Emma to a) stop speaking to her in a disrespectful way; b) reduce the amount of time she spent playing Minecraft; and c) help with the household chores.

Emma was a strong-willed, spirited kid who was not at all eager to accommodate her mom. When we brought up the topic of household chores, for example, Emma said, "Mom, you knew when you had me that it was going to be a lot of work. I'm just being a kid. You signed on for this; I don't know why I should have to help. You knew what you were getting into."

Twelve weeks later, Emma had reduced her Minecraft playing to acceptable levels, she was doing 25% of the household chores herself, and she was having productive, even sophisticated problem-solving conversations with her mom. They were now able to go on camping trips together, have friendly evenings at home, and Emma could be left alone at home for short periods of time. (These things weren't happening before the family called me.)

How did Emma do it? What did we do to help her to become so cooperative in just 12 weeks?

Well, in Emma's case I started with the assumption that she really did want to be helpful and loving toward her mom. Yes, she was very proud and very stubborn – autonomy was very important to her. She wanted to say what she did with her time and she didn't want anyone telling her she *had* to do anything. But she gave no indication of *disliking* her mom, or of wanting her mom to suffer. There was nothing in her behavior that suggested she wanted to sabotage the household.

So at first I tried to show Emma how she could nego-tiate with her mom and collaborate with her so that both parties could get what they needed. To Emma, though, this process represented a serious loss of control, and she refused to participate. So then we focused primarily on putting Mom back in charge of the family, which meant some pretty radical changes for Emma; loss of toys and clothes, whole days without Minecraft, and, of course, chores. And when she raged against all this, I asked her if she'd like to change it. "Of course!" she said. "I can't live like this!"

So I explained again how collaborative problem-solving worked, and I explained the Failproof Family Meeting. And this time around she was much more will-ing to respond to Mom's needs in a cooperative way. In the course of family-meeting conversations she came to agree that, as a person sharing a home, she should help with the housework. She was also able to come to an agreement about Minecraft time (she actually acknowledged that she knew she spent too much time playing).

The hardest part for this family was breaking through the entrenched communication habits that broke their connection and set mom and daughter against each other. Formal family meeting times were essential for these two, as the meetings were structured around completely different, positive communication patterns – and both parties understood the rules, and each person could help the other follow them.

And once Emma truly understood that she had a real say in the way the household operated, she became an enthusiastic participant. She even became a champion of her mom's free time, and insisted that her mom be able to take breaks, just like Emma did. Of course, in order for Mom to be able to take those breaks, they had to revisit the matter of chores, which resulted in Emma doing even more work than she had been doing.

And once Emma's mom believed that Emma was capable of cooperating and behaving rationally, her responses to Emma's impulsive behavior and prepubescent mood swings were less reactive and less emotional. Through family meetings, Emma and her mom had established new rules, protocols and communication patterns that suited both of them.

In this book I've given you my perspective as to what I think is the most effective way to help strong-willed kids become less oppositional and more cooperative. I've said that your perspective, your parenting mindset, is as important or even more important than your parenting techniques. I've said that parenting is much easier and more rewarding when you focus less on stopping undesired behavior and instead use your child's difficult behavior as an opportunity to develop and empower him. I've said that even though your child's behavior is more extreme than that of other kids, and even though parenting him has been difficult, there's absolutely nothing wrong with him – and it's important for you to see his strong will and stubbornness as very real strengths.

I've shared a few different perspectives and tools in this book, but the bottom line is this: *A happy family life requires both parents and kids to be empowered at the same time*. Parents need to be in charge of the family, and at the same time they need to relate to their child as a partner and collaborator. When everyone in the family knows they are going to be heard, people are more willing to listen. When everyone else in the family makes allowances for one person's differences, it makes that one person more willing to make allowances for others.

Consider the example of Emma. I wasn't exaggerating when I said that once she truly understood that she was able to help define the household rules, she became *much* more cooperative – even though this meant she would be doing things she had been completely unwilling to do before we started our work together.

It's pretty basic, really: Give respect to get respect. But spirited kids have a way of making that so difficult, it sometimes seems impossible. It sometimes seems that they *want* to make you late for work, they *want* to ruin the vacation, they *want* to get kicked out of school... But that's not true. Spirited kids want what every being wants: love and connection. They just have to be approached with a strength and a love that is as intense, deep, and relentless as they are. This can be exhausting, and it can be exhilarating. Don't expect to do it perfectly, and don't expect to do it alone. And give me a call if you'd like help. I'd love to be of support to you and your family.

ABOUT THE AUTHOR

Rebecah Freeling is a child behavior expert who specializes in children with impulsivity, emotional volatility, difficulty "listening," ADHD, aggression and bullying, and other behavior that's really, really challenging for parents, teachers – and other kids!

Rebecah owned and directed Briar Rose Children's Center, a highly-successful Waldorf-inspired early-childhood education center, from 1999-2011. These days she works primarily with families and schools, helping parents and kids to reduce stress and conflict in the home and helping schools and teachers to address disruptive behavior in the classroom. Rebecah received her education at Ohio State University and the Waldorf Institute of Southeast Michigan.

Rebecah is genuinely passionate about helping strong-willed, "spirited" kids develop self-discipline, social skills, and social responsibility. And one of her greatest joys is to help parents and schools create environments that turn children's weaknesses into strengths. Rebecah also loves kayaking, and cats.

PLEASE ACCEPT MY GIFT TO YOU!

Free Temperament Assessment ($400 value)

To help you understand your child better. This will ease your stress and frustration and it will help you to give your kids what they need to thrive!

Kids are not "blank slates," and not all kids are the same. You know that your kids have their own personality, but a formal assessment of your child's temperament will give you even more insight. It will help you to better understand your child, and it will help you to

- understand why your child does what he does
- understand which of your child's behaviors are normal and which are not
- not take "bad" behavior personally
- be more patient
- see the world from your child's perspective
- understand what motivates and inspires your child

Go to http://witsendparenting.com/tempassess to get started!

Made in the USA
Columbia, SC
15 October 2018